THE HUMAN IMPERATIVE

Planning
For People
In The
Electronic
Office

CONVERGING TECHNOLOGIES

THE HUMAN IMPERATIVE

Planning
For People
In The
Electronic
Office

MARY L. BAETZ

DOW JONES-IRWIN
HOMEWOOD, ILLINOIS 60430

Copyright © Holt, Rinehart and Winston of Canada, Limited

Published by Holt, Rinehart and Winston of Canada, Limited
Published simultaneously in the USA by Dow Jones-Irwin, Inc.,
1818 Ridge Road, Homewood, Illinois 60430

ISBN 0-87094-6528

Library of Congress Catalog Card No. 84-72804

Printed in Canada

To the one who insists I be all I can be.

Special thanks to Don Tapscott, Consulting Editor
and international authority in the field of integrated
office systems.

Contents

Acknowledgments

The acknowledgments section is the one part of the book which is written solely to meet the needs of the author rather than the reader. It would be impossible to write a book alone, many people share the effort and thanking them is a pleasurable duty. Not everyone's contribution can be mentioned, and for those who remain unnamed, please know that you are not forgotten.

The heroic efforts of my editor, Ingrid Philipp Cook, are largely responsible for this book's existence. Taking a concept and making it live is no easy task and for her diligence, support and caring I am deeply grateful.

Don Tapscott, creator of this series concept and longtime colleague, deserves special mention as well. He, and his partners at Trigon Technologies, Del Henderson and Morley Greenberg, have been tremendous contributors to the growth of interest in this field.

My sincere thanks to other colleagues who have helped the field develop and supported my growing involvement in it: Harvey Kolodny, Hans van Beinum, James Taylor, Sherm Grinnell, Dean Meyer and Cal Pava. Thanks go, as well, to my new friends from Holt, Rinehart and Winston, Carl Cross, Pat Slowey and Chris Marvin. Your patience and support is appreciated.

Those who reviewed the manuscript of this book made many insightful and constructive comments and, while I don't know all of your identities, I do thank every one of you, including Eric Lucking, Dave McGeown, Bryce Rutter and Keith Muller.

There are a number of special friends who shared the trials, challenged my theory-making and helped keep me going. My love and thanks go to Maureen Donlevy, Jessie Woodyatt, Mary Pearson, Marlene Potter, Pat Keating, Virginia Murray, Ingrid van Beinum, Marjorie Blackhurst and Anne Mellors, and, especially, to Roger and Sue Short.

And, above all, to the one who endured it all, I acknowledge my debt to Robin Wilson.

Mary Baetz
Toronto, 1984

Foreword

It is striking that many of the major problems that business has faced in taking advantage of new technology have not been technological. Rather than technical difficulties, it has been the inability or unwillingness to address the compelling human issues which has probably been the major cause of low productivity increases or even system failure.

This is particularly true in the office, where the introduction of new techology is precipitating far-reaching changes in the nature of work. As this technology matures to create the new "integrated office systems", the challenge of the "human imperative" becomes more critical.

Computer, office and telecommunications technologies are converging. The main product of this convergence is the electronic workstation — a microcomputer or terminal of some kind, networked to other technologies in the organization. The workstation provides an unprecedented tool for improving information handling, decisionmaking, communications and office administration. The advent of the personal business computer heralded the changes to come. Unlike traditional computer systems which were locked up in a data center, personal computers came to *directly support* all categories of office personnel — right up to the President. As the personal computer becomes a central part of the technical infrastructure in most organizations, its capabilities and impact are growing dramatically.

With this book, Mary Baetz has made an important contribution to bridging the gap between the potential of this technology and actual improvements in organizational performance. The gains today are slow, erratic and inconsistent. Diffusion of an innovation of this scope has been fraught with pitfalls which many of us never anticipated. For those organizations who have succeeded, the road has been rocky and full of surprises requiring considerable resources to resolve.

Management in general has been poorly equipped to grapple with this challenge. The issues are complex. There is little experience to rely upon. The threat of change has caused many to be resistant or to implement old ideas and methods of introducing technology and managing change. At worst, many computer systems have been designed along the lines of Frederick Taylor's 1885 Theory of Scientific Management. Taylor argued that a good work system was one where work was broken down into its individual tasks with one person, ideally, doing one task. Little variety in a job, strict monitoring of individual actions, extrinsic rewards, minimal responsibility and authority for most workers — to name a few — were all considered positive. One need only look to keypunch operators and wordprocessing centers as examples of contemporary applications of the Taylorist model. As a result, people in the office have often been the victims of technological change rather than the beneficiaries.

One would think that the Human Resources manager or executive would be a logical candidate to rise to the challenge of turning this situation around. Logic aside, this has generally not been the case. Fortunately, the Human Resources profession is now beginning to appreciate the implications of this "Third Wave" for their profession and their organizations.

This book will be a valuable asset for HR professionals and other managers who are interested in seeing office technology used effectively and humanely. Unlike many other discussions of the problems, the book is rooted in the author's experience in actually implementing these systems and managing change. One of the book's strengths is that, before jumping into the nitty gritty of the human resource problems, the author takes several chapters to establish a clear context and framework for the discussion.

A theme of the book is that there is no contradiction between planning for people, on the one hand, and using technology to improve productivity in the office, on the other. Rather, the two go hand-in-hand. It is becoming clear that the old Taylorist approach is not only lacking in humanity; it just doesn't work — especially when compared to new approaches to designing high performance work systems. In her book, Mary has outlined such a new approach to integrating people, technology and the physical environment for effectiveness.

In my opinion, those organizations which understand her message and can implement it will tend to succeed in optimizing their use of technology. With productivity, organizational performance, quality of work life, and corporate success and survival on the table, the stakes are high.

Don Tapscott
Consulting Editor
Converging Technologies Series
Toronto, June 1984

Preface

Today's manager is already well aware that the key issue for management in the 1980s is how to deal with the impact of microprocessor technology. The "Chip Revolution" has been the subject of innumerable articles, books, programs, seminars and courses. Its impact on the office and those who work in the office environment has also been dealt with at great length.

However, a crucial topic — how to manage within the context of this new microprocessor-based environment — has not been adequately addressed. Too often advice to managers and executives has been superficial and dogmatic: do this, don't do that. Little thoughtful discussion of the options available and the choices that will have to be made has occurred. Too often solutions have been presented when the reality is that we do not even know the proper definition of the problems we will be facing.

This book is intended to initiate an essential discussion. It is aimed at helping managers and other business professionals understand more fully the ways in which their professional lives will change as a result of the introduction of new technology in their organizations. It is meant as a lifeline to those who must now face the issues being raised by the introduction of new office technology, even while acknowledging the incompleteness of the theory base to deal with these issues. The environment will not wait for academia to catch up — you, and other managers must move forward and cope as best you can.

The intent is to encourage a thoughtful approach to the new office technology and its human impact so that readers will be more fully prepared to assist their organizations and themselves in meeting the coming challenges. They will be provided with a great deal of information so that they will be more able to interpret how the coming (and in some cases, already here!) changes will influence what their organization can do. They will be more able to predict possible opportunities which need to be taken advantage of. As well, they will be able to foresee potential trouble spots and take corrective actions to lessen the negative effects of change. There is no 'cookbook' approach that will be applicable in all cases — but you can learn enough to anticipate issues and begin to deal with them as they apply in your individual case.

The book can be read on a number of levels. When read from cover to cover, in order, the reader gains an overview of all the 'non-technical' aspects of the introduction of new office technology — how it affects the way we manage, what an 'ideal' implementation would involve, what the department or managers concerned with career planning, training, health and safety and office design might have to consider. On the other hand, for those who know *some* of these aspects already, you will learn more about how they interact with other aspects and other disciplines. For those who are designing systems and who are charged with implementing them, you will expand your knowledge of what to consider and who should be involved in the process.

There is no one best way when it comes to the electronic office. It all depends on the culture of the office, how far along people are in the use of various technologies, and on the kinds of behaviors that management wishes to reward and encourage. There are many choices to be made.

The task ahead of us was perhaps best stated by Roberto Assagioli in his book *The Act of Will* (New York: Penguin, 1973):

A specific, fundamental choice is *the choice between the past and the future*. We are in a period of drastic change and rapid renewal; many old forms do not work anymore. The old ways of life prove increasingly inadequate to meet present needs. Therefore, it is vain to remain attached to them and to delude ourselves by thinking that we can preserve them intact. On the other hand, the new is not to be chosen in a hurry and without discernment. At present, we are witnessing violent, excessive and ill-considered attempts to change everything at once. The renewal can and should be regulated by appropriate choices, wise decisions and a firm will. We should not abandon established ways without having found new and better ones. But once we have found the ways, we must have the courage and the will to throw ourselves boldly and joyfully into the adventure which the future holds.[1]

This book is about the choices available and the decisions that will have to be made.

Introduction

The Impact of Technology on People

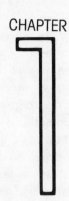

As a decisionmaker, you are betting your company's ability to function when the decision is made to introduce new technologies. You need to understand not only what the technological impact will be, but also how to *manage* its effect on your organization. It is no wonder that you want to know more about the possible effect of these new technologies on your people's productivity. After all, the enterprise exists to produce something — a product or service. If there is a chance that, through mismanagement, the "innovations" will harm, not help, their ability to produce, then you will want to deal with that possibility now.

The question, really, is not whether new office technologies will be introduced, as most organizations are beyond the point of no return on that issue. Their competitors have acquired office computers, individual employees are bringing in their own personal computers and home computers for office use, and requests for purchase are seen frequently. Rather, the question is how to ensure that the new technologies are brought in in such a way that the functioning of the *people* in your organization is enhanced rather than hindered. You do not want to become one of the many "horror stories" that show the reduction in productivity and morale that can accompany a badly managed move to the "office of the future". Examples of very high turnover, sabotage, and reduced ability to meet the customer's needs have made managers much more aware of the human issues involved in bringing technology into new settings. The management of these human issues is the topic of this book.

Let's start by looking at your own position. Since managers are, by and large, intelligent and thoughtful people who have learned to deal with a variety of issues, we'll assume that this description fits you. For the most part, your instincts have been developed over years of training and practice. When faced with a new opportunity, you try to relate it back to previous experience and base any decisions on your evaluation of the facts presented to support the argument.

But times have changed quite quickly and there are so many opportunities that are not easily related to past experience. In particular, many managers feel that they do not have good instincts in the area of the opportunities presented by new technology. They have no prior experience to give them a basis for evaluating the options. They feel there is something missing from the feasibility studies being presented to them, but can't quite put their finger on what that missing piece is. Their "expert advisers" speak with great confidence and promise many miracles. But their language is jargon-laden and the numbers are suspect. Internal advisers, perhaps the computer management staff, provide optimistic scenarios about 50 to a 100 percent increases in productivity and the external advisers, often computer salespeople, make promises of acceptance by the people and reductions in costs that are rarely appropriate and almost never included in the contract guarantees.

One way to fight the unease is to keep the problem in perspective. Yes, it is true that the introduction of new technology can be a time of massive organizational change. Yes, it is true that new skills will be needed and old skills may no longer be as applicable. But you have faced change before — organizations constantly reorganize, mergers and acquisitions occur, even entering a new enterprise or getting a promotion can be a massive change for the individual involved. The important thing for you, as a manager, is to learn in what ways this change is similar to others and in what ways it is different. You need to become familiar with where your managerial training will help you and where "old ways" may not be appropriate. This book will help you discover these distinctions and use them for your individual situation.

As managers search for ways to increase productivity, the focus is more often than not on how to deal with the human issues that can affect the ways in which people work. Management of other resources — money and capital investment — has become a well-developed skill. Now all managers are being called upon to increase their skills in handling their human resources. A few examples will help demonstrate some of the human issues that will need to be faced in some form in the near future.

- At an oil company, the Vice-President of Administration and Human Resources was put in charge of building a new corporate headquarters. Some questions he needed to deal with were: What spaces are needed now and for the next twenty years? Which offices and working spaces should be equipped to handle the new technologies, some of which are not even invented? How will jobs and employees change and what impact will this have on the design of this new building?
- At an office technology divisional sales office, new word-processing

equipment was installed. Within six months of the installation, there was 100 percent turnover within the support staff. Since this office serviced salespeople selling this same equipment to organizations, it was an extremely embarrassing and untenable situation. The office manager faced the challenge of redesigning the jobs and recruiting new operators in such a way that not only met the needs of the office, but also allowed salespeople to again assure their would-be clients that the equipment would not create problems during introduction.

- At a union headquarters, the President of the union had to respond to demands that service be increased at no additional cost to members and to requests for the new office technology made by employees of the union. This same union had taken a public stand to resist the introduction of microprocessor-based technology at all organizations in which it had a local.

These are all very difficult cases. But who is to say that you won't face an equally difficult problem. The new technology, particularly office technology, is presenting us with undreamed opportunities — and with nightmare-like problems.

The Myth of the Peopleless Office

When computer-based office systems first made their appearance, a common prediction foretold of the "dawn of the era of the paperless office". We now know that the paperless office is not only an unrealizable dream, but one not even worth pursuing. More recently, there has been a lot written about the impact of office technologies on employment and a new "era" seems to be visualized, one in which people are no longer needed in offices.

For some managers, this seems a good turn of events. If technology can replace people, then let's take it to the extreme and eliminate everyone. After all, machines don't take coffee breaks or ask for raises and vacations. And we all know that most of the problems relating to the use of technology come from people resisting it and sabotaging its introduction. Therefore, let's replace all these troublesome people with non-complaining machines.

But, of course, if life were that simple, there would be no need for managers either. The office, more than any other part of the organization, needs people to handle a constantly varying influx of information from all sources: proposed and new legislation from all levels of government, new products and services available from competitors, new demands from consumers, new ideas and tools from research and development organizations, and all the information generated from within the organization. The productivity of the entire enterprise relies on the ability of those in the office to analyze the changing demands of the environment and to assist all parts with their adaptation to the new demands. The ability to integrate the information and evaluate it within the context of the organization's goals and plans and then make decisions and carry out actions based on this analysis is not within the capabilities of any machine now available on any basis. Office technology can ease the load, indeed may be required to handle the load, but it cannot and will not replace the human contribution in the near future.

This, then, makes your managerial skills all the more important to your organization. People are crucial to the successful implementation of new technology and management is crucial to their acceptance. Management of people is a vital skill that office technologies cannot replace and the manager who succeeds will be the one who recognizes this fact. As we will see shortly, becoming "computer literate" is the latest fad; I argue that those who spend time on becoming "human literate" will find their skills even more highly valued within their organization.

You will be dealing with many other managers in your organization who, like yourself, will most likely respond to the new technologies in one of three ways. Some will reject the introduction of new office technology altogether. This is phrased in many ways: "Wait until the new generation of equipment appears" or "We can't go forward until we are sure all the equipment will work together" or "Our customers see us as conservative and reliable, we don't want to destroy that image."

Another response is to put one's trust in the advisers: "We must go forward or be left behind by our competitors" or "We have our image as leading-edge to maintain." The optimism of the advisers is accepted and supported, the horror stories are viewed the way smokers view cancer statistics — it can't happen here.

A third approach, becoming more common, is to put the decision on "hold" while the managers become "computer literate", that is, learn how to program computers. Of course, few of us want to appear "illiterate", so we see the emergence of computer camps for adults and computer classes at resorts such as Club Med. Here is an opportunity to learn outside of the organization environment.

All of these responses have benefits and drawbacks. If you refuse to join the "office of the future", upheaval at the office is avoided and business can proceed as usual. However, this is only true in the short run.

You may indeed be losing out to your competitors as your productivity declines and your ability to respond to the needs of your clients is eroded.

If, instead, you dive into the technology, your organization will gain valuable experience and at least some of your employees will get access to information that will upgrade decisionmaking. But you may be faced with a revolt among the workers, and if the technology is not properly introduced, integrated and maintained, you may have less, not more, information available.

And, of course, you will need some skills in using the technology in the years ahead. But becoming "computer literate" requires more than taking programming courses and using personal computers. Your ability to assess the impact of the technology options presented by your advisers will depend on your understanding of the technology's potential impact on how the business operates, how people will use the machines and what your competitors are doing. The early 1900s provide a most helpful analogy, that of the automobile. In this case, successful managers had to see the impact of the automobile on the structure and functioning of the economy. They could not learn this just by learning to drive a car, however necessary that new skill was going to be to them personally. Certainly, they did not need to learn to maintain the car, but rather they needed to know enough about the basic principles of a safely functioning vehicle to know when to seek help.

With respect to the new technology, each of us must first learn to be comfortable using (not programming) the equipment. Second, we need to develop people who can maintain the equipment to whom we can turn for assistance. And, equally importantly for management, each must increase his or her own understanding of the long-term and far-ranging effects of this very real change to our economic and social structure. "Computer literacy" has a very different meaning when considered this way.

These rather simple responses — opt out, abdicate to specialists, or delay — grow out of the frustration that managers and executives feel when faced with the need to decide major issues when they have ambiguous and contradictory information and little historical precedent on which to base their evaluations. This book will provide these decision-makers with information and examples that will help them feel more confident of their own ability to understand the issues and be sure that they are receiving the appropriate information and analyses from their support systems. Only then can they choose the response that is truly appropriate for their organization.

Beyond Jargon

A major stumbling block for managers is the jargon used by office automation professionals. All jargon is developed to convey useful thoughts
in a shorthand that allows fast, efficient communication among those
"in the know". The problem appears when the jargon is then carried
over into communication with the "uninitiated". Jargon can then make
people feel uneducated and useless. They hesitate to contribute to con-
versations or make decisions that involve the technology referred to by
this jargon.

Where computer-based jargon is concerned, we have an even more
interesting problem. Not only do the professionals sometimes take
common, everyday terms and give them new, specifically technical
meanings; they also reduce everything to initials so that we have to deal
with two levels of jargon!

When "computer literate" people start to discuss computer-related
topics, they quickly lapse into bits and bytes, systems, and ROMs, RAMs,
and LANs. The terms sound meaningful, yet to the"average" person
make no sense in the context in which they are used. The important
thing to remember is that you, as a manager, should not have to understand the jargon in order to understand the discussion. You would demand that a doctor or lawyer use common English to explain their
positions; you can demand the same of other professionals working for
you. Jargon is useful only to those who have to deal with the concepts
every day.

**Whether your people, and you, can do what is required more easily, more
competently, and more flexibly with the tools you have chosen is the only
question that should concern you.**

We will be exploring the various effects of the introduction of new office
technology and the opportunities it presents. So it is important that we
share common definitions of the tools and processes at which we will be
looking.

The choice of language is often an indication of the orientation of the
writer or speaker. For example, there are various phrases that have been
used to describe the new office technology. These include "the automated office", "the office of the future", "the computer-mediated office",
and "the integrated office". But "automated" expresses the feeling of
being "robotized" or "mechanized" in some way and "the office of the
future" is with us already. "Computer-mediated", while a good academic
term because of its conciseness, is not sufficiently accepted in business to

be used here. "Integrated office" expresses the concept that the various components of office technology must work together somehow to achieve a desired end.

A variation on the term "integrated office" is "integrated office systems". While not yet perfect because it does not highlight sufficiently the central importance of people, this is the phrase I prefer to use when referring to the office technologies that we are considering. This phrase directs attention to the key components which must be considered. First, it is the office which is the focal point. The office is the "brain" of an organization. Its fundamental resource is information and its central products are decisions to be communicated and acted upon. The *people* within and without the office are the ones who make and act upon these decisions — therefore, neither the resource (information) nor the products (decisions) are relevant without reference to the people.

Second, we are concerned with all of the systems in the office. While the word "systems" has become synonymous with computer systems, in fact, systems has a much broader meaning. A system includes the people, procedures, skills, physical plant, and tools which characterize a unit or an organization.

Third and most importantly, it is the integration and interdependence of all the systems that is fundamental to success. This recognizes that any intervention which affects one of the systems, affects all of the systems. Therefore you cannot afford to have any analysis of any office automation taking place in a vacuum.

An integrated office results, then, from the bringing together of tools and structures which enhance people's ability to make and implement decisions. For the most part, the new emphasis is on electronic tools and computer-based structures. Actually, the office, in most organizations, has been functioning (and "integrated", that is, with the various parts working well together, to some degree) for a long period of time. It is the introduction of the newly available electronic technologies, and the need to "reintegrate" all the office systems (human as well as technical) that is the driving force for organizational change now. The introduction of technology, like any other change in the office system, interrupts the working together of other parts and these need to be realigned so that all parts are, once again, in harmony.

The new office technologies or integrated office systems, are not, I must emphasis, limited to word processing. Word processing involves using a microprocessor-based machine which increases a person's ability to easily change the words or the structure of a written piece. While this is a useful tool, it is merely one out of many available.

So exactly what new dimensions are to be added by the new technologies? The new electronic equipment allows people to gather information available inside the organization or from the outside, to create documents, to communicate without regard to geographical location or time differences, and to reorganize the information to make it more easily understood.

This equipment is the result of a merger of three kinds of technologies. First are those text management technologies which help the person to create, edit and reproduce text. They are called word processing or text editing tools. Most offices have other text management tools such as typewriters and copiers. Second are those technologies which help the person to manipulate numbers. These may be statistical packages or financial modeling tools; other office tools of the same nature are calculators and large computer systems. Finally, there are those technologies which help the person deal with communications. These include electronic mail and other computer-based messaging systems, electronic telephones, and private branch exchanges (PBXs) which are the telephone switching systems for individual organizations.

Taken individually, these do not seem new or startling enough to be worth all the attention being paid to them. And, indeed, if they were separate items, any organization would introduce them over time and absorb them very easily. But these are not separate items. The new technologies can be brought together into integrated office systems. These enable each person to switch back and forth among the various components in ways that were never before possible. Using them aggressively, each person can enhance her or his effectiveness significantly.

Various other tools can be added to further enhance productivity. These include graphics packages which allow the person to communicate numerical information pictorially using charts and graphs, filing systems which allow the person to have access to any relevant information, and calendaring systems that allow one to manage one's time better. In addition there are several ways which enable a number of people to communicate simultaneously despite being separated by distance.

All of these capacities are available now. Even more will be available in the future. The rate of introducing new or improved tools is increasing and everyone in every organization is being affected. This new reality is causing managers like yourself to treat the functioning of the office as a strategic issue in organizational success.

Managing Change

There is another critical confluence which will cause concerned managers to reevaluate the way in which they have been dealing with problems and opportunities. As we will see in Chapter Two, the technological revolution is but one factor. Other influences include the changing demographic makeup of the work force caused by the aging of the baby boom generation and the increase in participation by women, older persons and the disabled; the emergence of the "post-industrial society" (admittedly microprocessor-based); and the transition taking place on the economic front. All of these converge to create an organizational world in which yesterday's rules do not apply and old theories are less relevant or need to be used in innovative ways.

If this is the case, then why focus on office technology? Because it is during the introduction of change, such as that caused by the implementation of new office technology, that managers are forced to realize the need for changes in their own assessments of what works and why. As will become obvious in later chapters, human resource management will be reaching into new areas in most organizations. The successful integration of the management of all resources — human, physical, informational, financial and technical — is the key to organizational effectiveness in the 1980s and 1990s.

We know that the new technology will lead to an eventual restructuring of the organization. As the various tools are integrated and the organization uses information in innovative ways, new methods of working and relating will emerge. It is impossible to predict the final patterns ahead of time; but we know the old ones won't do. In order to continue to optimize the use of the organization's resources, there will be a push to restructure. Recognition of this fact allows managers and executives to plan for the changes coming and to plan for the management of these changes.

A major source of frustration for managers is the lack of clear data about the impact of office technology on people. Many scare stories have been published in newspapers and magazines or told at meetings. On the other hand, there is a concerted effort by the vendors of equipment and the specialists who recommend and install equipment to downplay the possiblity of any negative impact on people.

In this book we look at the factors that affect the way in which people do their work and how these factors are influenced by the introduction of new office systems. We will explore the possible outcomes of various methods of introduction and will present scenarios to help decision-makers feel confident that the impact of technology on employees is being properly considered in any analysis of the acquisition of office systems.

To put the issues in perspective, we must examine the environment from which you draw your employees and see how this environment is changing. The shifting makeup of the work force — increasing education level, changing values, different age categories, and rising expectations for quality of life — will affect what you, as an employer, can and cannot expect to do with respect to the new technologies and the changes they bring. The impact of the transformation of the economy from industrial base to information base and the increasingly important role of the multinational will also place new demands on you.

The introduction of an office system is a major shock to the organization. There are many ways to ease the shock and help ensure that promised gains can be realized. But these ways are not always known to the systems or administrative people so often given responsibility for bringing in new office systems. Chapter Four begins our look at implementation and introduces the concept that, far from being a point in time long after the planning process begins,

implementation of integrated office systems begins when the first manager begins to think about the possibilities of increasing productivity in the office.

This simple fact is often overlooked and many avoidable problems flow from this oversight. In the earliest stages of systems consideration, decisions are made, attitudes are formed, and actions are taken that can seriously affect the organization's acceptance of new technology.

The actual introduction of new office technology can be a time of crisis for an organization if this introduction is not handled well. A good deal of planning is called for. In particular, how management communicates what is happening and will happen to people, jobs, and the organization will have a significant effect on how well people accept the technology. In addition, there is a need to "manage success", for if expectations and enthusiasms are raised and not met, the results can set back the implementation.

The number and variety of management issues to be considered indicate that planning for the implementation of office systems must be systematic, comprehensive and integrative. There needs to be involvement, in the actual planning process, of representatives of all the people who will be affected. Clearly, this is "strategic planning" at its most fundamental level.

Yet, a major current dilemma for most staff departments is how to ensure the needed integration of the various plans with the overall strategic planning process of the organization. Too often, each staff group is faced with implementing a plan in whose design they have had no meaningful involvement. It is evident that an organization's ability to carry out any strategies will depend on its ability to understand the impact of new technology on its functioning. The Human Resources and Systems departments, in particular, will need to educate the rest of the organization concerning these issues.

Throughout the implementation process and long afterwards, you will be asking specific questions about the management of people during this time of change. I have tried to anticipate these and in Parts Three and Four give guidance as to possible approaches to the resolution of these questions. The changes present new challenges to traditional managers and traditional management processes. With the trend to more information processing and less production of tangible items, quality control becomes more difficult and it is not easy to assess the performance of people. When employees work variable hours and from different locations, as is possible using the new systems, it is hard to establish how the work is being done (at least according to more traditional measures). New evaluation criteria and methods of data collection are required when new technology is introduced which will be used by professionals and managers.

Job design has a profound impact on motivation and organizations have found that the intelligent design or redesign of jobs as they are "automated" has made the difference in experiencing the gains promised from the technology. Each organization will have to face the issue of what to do with the people whose jobs have been eliminated as a result of the introduction of new technology. For those organizations which choose to retain the people made redundant (recognizing the skills, organizational knowledge and energy which these people have), the task of retraining these people must be faced. This will not be a one-time problem, as the technology will continue to change and jobs will go out of existence on an ongoing basis. Of course, new jobs and new job categories will also be created constantly and many organizations will use these opportunities to design jobs that will retain and motivate the employees previously affected.

The issues of job design are closely related to those of the physical design of the space in which the job must be performed. When introducing new office technologies, you must consider the way the physical layout of the office enhances or interferes with the well-being of employees (from both the physical and psychological perspectives).

Training departments will have tremendous demands placed upon them during the introduction of new office systems. The users are the first concern and continuous training of them will be an ongoing challenge. Both supervisors and managers (whether they are users or not) will need assistance in learning to delegate more to their subordinates and in learning to "package" work so that it can be successfully accomplished by those using the new technology. The entire organization will need to be educated as to what impacts can be expected from new technology and what the organization's response will be.

The new technology will have significant implications for the way people work. Indeed, the definition of "work" will change, and the distinction between work and non-work (including productive contribution) will blur. Alternative patterns of work will evolve and organizations must understand how to effectively use these patterns to improve productivity and quality of working life for these employees.

All of this will make career planning even more difficult than it is now. Indeed, the concept of "career", as well as the concept of "work", will need to be reconsidered. With some career paths being closed off and others emerging (because of the new technology) and with alternative work patterns, everyone in the organization will need assistance in learning a new form of career planning.

Another dilemma is presented: how will we reward employes who are working in innovative ways, perhaps not on-site, perhaps not producing a tangible product, and probably performing jobs which those who must establish the rewards are not able to understand fully? With regard to people working at home or on alternate work schedules, the temptation will be to reward for product produced (when available, such as lines typed) or for hours signed on the machine when there is no tangible product. But the former is a return to the "piecework" system that is now rejected by most people and the latter is not a valid measure of contribution or performance. You, as a decisionmaker, need to understand and evaluate the problems and opportunities in the compensation and appraisal areas.

Throughout the book a number of issues will be raised for which there are no easy solutions, and, indeed, about which too little may be known to even phrase the question fully. Yet the responsibility for dealing with these problems will fall to management anyway. Decisions about policies on health and safety aspects or on job design issues will need to be made. If you are able to see these issues clearly, you will at least have taken the crucial first step to understanding, planning for and managing them. And this, indeed, is the point. There are many areas which will be affected by integrated office systems, but it is the management of the human issues that cannot be automated and the manager who wants to keep managing will take the time to learn this.

THE NEW REALITIES

1

The Changing World

"Unstable", turbulent", "unpredictable" and "unmanageable" are words used by managers to depict the business world they now face. Not only are there many changes taking place simultaneously, but the communication of them has speeded up enormously. In addition, they interact in such a way to produce further, unpredicted shifts with which all must cope. While we will examine some of these changes and make some predictions as to their impact, we must never lose sight of the fact that the major management task of the future is to prepare the employees of the organization to deal in a mature, purposive manner with the unpredictability which they will constantly face.

It is important to understand how business itself will change in order to understand the way in which the management of business (which is, in fact, the purpose of the office) must also adapt. One clear example from the manufacturing side of the coming changes is that of the "Workerless Factory" made possible by the creation of Flexible Manufacturing Systems (FMS). These systems rely on the integration of computer-based technology with machining equipment, use computer-aided design (CAD), robots, computer-assisted quality control centers (CAQ), and computer-controlled parts delivery and warehousing support systems.

The true impact is not related to the absence of workers, though this is important in itself. The most important point is that FMS allows for the production of small lots (even single items) with the economies of scale previously associated with mass production. Because FMS is based on computer-operated machines which can be easily and quickly reprogrammed, the manufacturing process can instantly adapt to new demands from the marketplace. As noted in a *Fortune* magazine article, "Flexible manufacturing is the ultimate entrepreneurial system; it will allow fast-thinking manufacturers to move swiftly into brand-new fields and to leave them just as swiftly if need be — at the expense of less agile older producers."[1]

Currently there is a generation of managers trained in and rewarded for applying the best of Scientific Management Theory (where all production, office as well as factory, is simplified to the extreme and then closely supervised) and working its way down the "experience curve" (so named because it represents a curve showing that higher production leads to increased experience that allows a manufacturer to make changes that reduce the costs of production). For these individuals, the change in behavior and attitude needed to become the entrepreneur of the future is awesome. Yet, clearly, this is the environment which will be the context for management in the years ahead.

Again we return to the theme that

management's key task is to become flexible and able to respond appropriately and positively to turbulence in the environment.

For every organization, the specifics will be different — for a manufacturing company it may mean acquiring flexible manufacturing systems. For a service company it may mean having in place a training group capable of quickly training all employees to provide the new services constantly being introduced to meet changing market demands. In all companies, it will mean having sufficient information to be able to react quickly to changing market demands and unexpected opportunities. Data will be available from both internal and external sources in astonishing amounts and you will need to be able to extract from it information which is useful and relevant to your organization's needs, abilities and plans. All companies will have to build in the capacity to respond; therefore, flexibility is key whether talking of people, systems, plant, or procedures.

The Information Society

Each organization must learn how it is affected by the major shift that is taking place in the structure of the world economy. This shift has been variously referred to as the "Age of the Microprocessor" or the "Post-Industrial Era" or the "Information Society". Each of these titles reflects some of the flavor of the change — none captures it fully.

In reality, we are going through a transformation equivalent to that experienced when the Western world shifted from an agricultural to an industrial based economy. The microprocessor (and those technologies which will replace the microprocessor but perform similar functions) is, indeed, the tool which allows this transformation to proceed. But to call it the "Age of the Microprocessor" is to focus on the tool of the change and miss the major significance of the change.

While some countries will continue to be dependent on agriculture for their economic survival, there is little debate that those countries that are predominantly industrial will face massive changes in their economic makeup in the next few decades. For example, the Rand Corporation predicted in 1982 that employment in manufacturing will drop from the current 20 percent of the work force in the United States to 2 percent of the work force in twenty years.

Of course, a decline in employment is no longer synonymous with a decline in production. Much of the manufacturing that will take place will be done in factories using new technologies, such as robots, that allow fewer people to produce increased amounts of goods. But, in the last few years we have seen the growth of the information sector of the economy in terms of employment and gross sales, with the service sector becoming dominant. So we already are in the "Post-Industrial Era".

The final phrase noted, "The Information Society", most fully captures the nature of the transformation. It shows that the change goes beyond the economy to the level of society itself. Increasingly, managers recognize that management of information is a requirement for success at the individual, organizational and national level. But information is an "ethereal good" — that is, it is not consumed when used nor is its value easily computed because the cost of "production" is so difficult to establish. So we can assume that appropriate approaches to this resource management challenge will not be derived directly from those used to control the production of tangible goods.

What does it mean, then, to "manage information" on various levels? It begins with the understanding that people seek to understand and ultimately control what is happening around them. As the uncertainty and unpredictability of the world is increased, people and organizations demand more and more bits of data so that they can have a feeling of more certainty about their decisions and about the consequences of their actions.

In addition, the very existence of new technologies makes it possible for more data to be collected, digested and analyzed, which in turn increases the demand for information because, of course, everyone wants to know anything a competitor might know. And, finally, as people have higher levels of education than in the past, they are more comfortable with collecting and analyzing information, rather than relying on the interpretations of others. In combination these three forces (economic, technological and demographic) place great pressure on organizations to provide increasing amounts of information to individuals (either at their homes or at work), to other organizations and to institutions such as governments.

So it is that the organization that can respond to these demands, in other words, that can successfully manage information, will be the more successful organization because it is meeting consumers and regulators needs most responsively and at the least cost. Consumers are increasingly willing to pay for information as a product. One example of this is the use of external databases, which charge on the basis of use. Many of these databases contain reports, statistics, and articles that are available for free from libraries. Yet the subscribers are willing to pay for more convenient access to these. In addition, we are seeing that consumers will pay if information is added to an existing product, such as the "navigation centers" available as an option on some cars, and for the quality which is an outcome of attention paid to the information component of the production process. It is no secret that much of the reputation for quality that the Japanese have created is due to their learning how to use production data to decrease component failure rates and to increase quality without increasing costs.

On the other hand, the increasing demands for information by the organization's suppliers such as banks, insurance companies and the various levels of government are putting a burden on the organization. Those which are structured to be able to provide reports and statistics quickly and with little disruption will find themselves more competitive than those organizations which have not made these changes. These "outside" forces are in addition to the intraorganizational forces which are the more common rationale for increasing the organization's ability to manage information.

These demands for information do not stop at national boundaries. Because information is intangible, it easily crosses borders and cultures. With the new translation programs being developed, it will be possible to have information produced and instantly available in all markets. Thus, organizations and managers in this new era must increasingly think of their markets in worldwide terms.

The Changing Workforce

The major benefit that information bestows upon an organization is an increased ability to respond to changing demands. This brings us back again to the importance of flexibility in the organizations of the future. But if flexibility is an important component of success, so are the people on whom we will depend to provide this component. We can not rely on luck and chance to ensure that we have the employees we need to prosper in the future.

The workforce is undergoing a major transformation. Employees of the 1980s and 1990s are qualitatively different from employees of the past. These differences are evident in such easily observed factors as education and skill levels, age distribution and percentages of women working, as well as from the less obvious, such as values espoused. We will take each in turn.

The Baby Boom, having created upheaval in the school and university systems, is now having the same effect on organizations. The impact of a large number of people entering the workforce simultaneously would be profound anytime. But this group is also the best educated and the first to be raised with television. They bring to the workplace a set of skills which used to be found only in a minority of employees. There is another view, which says that the young people emerging from school now are less educated than their predecessors because of the pernicious influence of television and the failure of the school systems to educate. Both views probably have some validity; what we *do* know is that the number of years of schooling has increased for the majority and so is no longer a good criterion on which to select for management positions.

In the "old days", the people who ran organizations tended to be those who also had the most education. This created a belief that education leads to promotion. But now, the majority of the workforce has attained the education level that was primarily for the few in the past. The new reality is that since a majority has significantly increased its educational level, education no longer provides a competitive boost up the corporate ladder. But this reality has not been perceived by all. Needless to say, there will be a lot of dashed expectations.

Another factor which will lead to many people being disappointed in their rate of promotion is the age distribution of the workforce. Those born during the Baby Boom (defined as the years 1946-61 in the U.S. and 1951-66 in Canada) are now first encountering the rapid narrowing of the organizational pyramid. The group born just prior to the Baby Boom was abnormally small; so those who entered the workforce from this group had lots of opportunities, little competition and most moved up rapidly. Such expectations — the belief that one's high education level and that the experience of the managers who preceeded indicates how one's own career will proceed — is now unrealistic.

Also contributing to the changing workforce is the increasing partici- pation of women. The rate of women working has increased steadily from the 1950s on, approximates 50 percent now and will most likely be about 75 percent by early in the next century. As females are slightly more than 50 percent of the total population, this means that the work force will be close to 40 percent female as opposed to about 25 percent now. These women will have the same education level as men and will expect equal job treatment. They will be less likely to stay home after the birth of a child and will be looking for careers, not jobs. They, too, face disappointment. The typical career path, in any organization, will undergo radical change. Our experience of the past will not be a very good guide to the future.

While the effect of demographics is very important, the effect of changing value systems will have a much greater impact on the way we manage in the future. An excellent analysis of popular current values is provided by Daniel Yankelovich in his book *New Rules: Searching for Self-Fulfillment in a World Turned Upside Down*. The title is itself an indication of the value shift. As he says:

> On traditional demands for material well-being seekers of self-fulfillment now impose new demands for intangibles — creativity, leisure, autonomy, pleasure, participation, community, adventure, vitality, stimulation, tender loving care. To the efficiency of technological society they wish to add joy of living. They seek to satisfy both the body and the spirit, . . . Why, they argue, should we accept as inevitable that resourceful, highly educated people have to choose between the efficiency of technological society and quality of life?[2]

These seekers of self-fulfillment bring to the employment setting new expectations. They seek work which not only provides a living, but also provides an opportunity to grow. They seek to optimize the quality of their lives, and see work as an integral component in this search. No longer will they compartmentalize their lives and accept a dull, repetitive, spirit-killing job and live out their hopes and dreams in their leisure hours. It is not only North Americans who feel this way. The noted social systems analyst Eric Trist notes that "Attitude surveys in several countries indicate that only the older worker continues to be willing to trade off dehumanizing work simply for good wages and employment security."[3]

In truth, previous generations have all desired "self-fulfillment". And those of means were often able to attain it. The difference is that this generation insists that they be allowed to satisfy their desires for growth and development through their work. The decision to split one's life — tolerate the job in order to have the family life, home, and hobbies that provide personal satisfaction — is being supplanted by the search for ways to integrate all aspects of one's life. So viewed, it can be seen as a healthly response to what was previously an unhealthy situation.

The problem is that employees are trying to change "the rules of the game" at a time when organizations are also undergoing other massive strains on their way of doing business. This creates a strain that can result in rejection of the values that the employees bring and failure to recognize that the changes requested can actually assist the organization to cope with other changes. This is because

the new ways of working being sought are, by definition, creative, flexible, innovative and proactive — just the employee traits organizations need to cultivate to be responsive to their environment.

Another area to which enterprises must pay attention is the response of institutions to the changing environment. By institutions, I mean those organizations which represent various slices of society: unions, various levels of government, schools and universities, special interest groups (such as women, the disabled, and ethnic minorities) to mention a few. Even while outside the business sphere (though many are also businesses in their own right), they often create social change through their influence on the legislative process, social pressure, or contracts which have a direct impact on an organization's ability to conduct its affairs as it sees fit.

We have some information about how unions will respond both to the general turbulence in the economy and to the specific impact of technology. Unions have typically been most active in improving working conditions for those who are employed and in protecting the jobs of members. Thus their focus has traditionally been to negotiate contracts which enhance health and safety, job security and pay. For the most part their appeal has been to those workers whose jobs were dangerous or insecure and perceived as underpaid and who would most likely have difficulty moving to another kind of employment. They negotiate for workers who feel they need help in negotiating with their more powerful bosses.

But consider the environment that has been outlined so far. Workers are more educated and their background is more like their employer's. They feel more powerful. They are interested in growth and development, not an area in which unions have traditionally taken an active interest. They may feel their jobs are not very secure, but feel they have the ability to move on to other fields if need be — indeed, the concepts of life-long learning and multiple careers has already been accepted by them. They will be, for the most part, working in non-manufacturing settings, thus feeling less fear for their physical safety. There is the worry over possible negative effects from long-term exposure to VDTs, which we will look at in a later chapter, but, in general, it is clear that immediate health hazards are less common.

The industries in which unions have the strongest position at this time are those very same industries which are most likely to experience declines in the future; these are the manufacturing-based industries, which grew through the exploitation of the economies of scale produced by mass production. One example will illustrate the combined impact of the new economy, new technology, and the recent recession on union membership.

The United Steelworkers of America have in the past decade experienced a continual decline in membership, exacerbated in recent years by the recession. In 1974 the union had 1.4 million members. In 1981, after a period of growth and increasing employment for the economy as a whole, the membership had declined slightly to 1.2 million. In the next year the union was effectively cut in half as membership at the end of 1982 stood at only 688,000 and was still dropping. The Canadian portion of the membership decline was somewhat less severe than the American portion, moving from 197,000 to 125,000 in the 1981-82 period.

While dramatic, this example is far from unique. The organizations most likely to have a substantial union component are also those which are seen as being in the "sunset" industries. The "sunset" industries are those which are mature and perhaps also in decline, because of foreign competition and reduced demand. These include steel, auto, rubber, and other manufacturing companies, to name a few. Emerging growth industries, in contrast, are known as "sunrise" and include telecommunications and other high technology areas. These tend to be employers of white-collar clerical and professional workers (often referred to collectively as "knowledge workers") who are least likely to be union members. If represented at all, these workers tend have professional societies and employee groups rather than traditional unions. What unions we find among knowledge workers generally are not militant. If the more powerful unions continue to lose membership and the emergent ones proceed according to historical patterns, there is little expectation that they will be a force in North America in the future. In fact, one well-known futurist, John Naisbitt, has predicted that the U.S. is moving towards an almost "union-free" society.

But, of course, union leaders are able to see the trends and are now taking proactive stances to ensure that unions survive and if possible thrive, in the next few decades. One way to do this is to change the basic appeal of unions; that is, to move from apppealing to the basic needs for survival and security to demonstrating that they can be responsive to the desire of members for growth and development. Unfortunately, only a few leading-edge union heads have taken this stance.

The more typical union reaction to the opportunity presented by office automation has been to approach the office as if it were a factory. That is, they continue to focus on issues of health and safety, job security and negotiating power. The reaction has been mixed. In the recession, there was some sympathy for the issue of job protection during the introduction of new technology. And the current confusion over the impact of VDTs on health has led some workers to request protection. But, in most cases, the employees have felt sufficiently powerful, or have not seen that the unions have enough to add, so that unions have not been perceived as the vehicle through which employees wish to address their dissatisfaction should there, in fact, be any.

However, there are indications that the union movement might be more successful in the future. As in any other organization, unions are increasingly managed by people who are themselves Baby Boomers, sharing the same values as the employees they wish to unionize. Up until now, the hierarchy of most unions had been through the trials-by-fire of the earlier days and were reluctant to change the appeals that had worked for them. The new generation of union organizers will be more likely to respond in a positive way to the changing needs of the new employee. With this approach, the new breed has the potential to increase overall union membership and to work with management, through the collective bargaining process, to develop innovative plans to increase the overall quality of working life for employees.

We know that many groups try to influence legislation which affects the use of new technology at all organizational levels. In Europe, there have been laws enacted which prescribe the design of workstations, the number of hours employees can work on video display terminals, and which require that employees be notified of any plans to introduce new technology, before the purchases are made. In Canada, similar legislation has been introduced at both the provincial and federal level. This legislation has not yet been passed.

It is not always the unions that push for legislation. A number of special interest groups have sprung up to carry the banner for unorganized as well as organized workers. Those who work for the cause of women in the workplace include, in the U.S., 9 To 5 - National Association of Office Workers, and, in Canada, the Canadian Advisory Council on the Status of Women and the Canadian Congress for Learning Opportunities for Women. These and other groups work to educate the public and to influence legislation in this area. Of course, there are also groups which represent computer manufacturing companies (such as the American and Canadian Business Equipment Manufacturers Associations) trying to influence the direction any such legislation takes.

The major focus of these groups is to impress upon the lawmakers where it is necessary to create uniform standards for the use of technology. Not surprisingly, we find that legislated standards may not be in the best interests of some organizations. As with all laws, the creation of one limits the rights of some group in order to protect the rights of another.

It is difficult and time-consuming to legislate change. But, of course, there are many other ways to influence the way organizations function. Groups such as unions are using the collective bargaining or contracting process; many new contracts already include requirements for consultation regarding plans for new technology and job security for individuals affected by the introduction of technology.

To be successful within this political environment, you, as a manager, must learn the kinds of legislation and private contracts that are being proposed and understand the reasons for the demands contained within them.

Many of the demands are an outgrowth of previous management ignoring the needs of the employees and failing to respond to real problems that have been created by the introduction of new technology. As is so often the case, the demands can be an over-reaction to previous abuse and end up punishing the more progressive management along with the abusers. But, for you, the need is to foresee possible constrictions on your ability to manage and to do your best to ensure that your organization is flexible enough to manage despite restrictions. Many of the organizations mentioned publish their stands on issues such as new technology, quality of work life efforts (QWL) and joint labor-management committees. For example, the United Steelworkers of America recently published *Towards A Trade Union Agenda* which provides a good background on the union stance regarding QWL initiatives.[4]

Understanding the environment is a necessary requirement for managing the impact it can have on your organization. With the astounding amount of data available, the ability to synthesize and draw meaning from it all is a skill which every manager must develop. To reject the information because it seems overwhelming or unmanageably complex will not make its impact go away. It merely guarantees that you will always remain in a reactive state.

The Business of Tomorrow

Changes in the corporate environment require organizations to evolve or become less effective competitors. The integrated office technology is both a driving factor in this evolution and a key component of the coping strategy that most organizations will choose.

Analysis of the larger picture — the shifting structure of the economy, the need to compete internationally in the new global market, and the need to be able to quickly fill consumer demands as they change — tells us that corporations and other organizations will need to be structured in such a way that they can respond to the changing demands and interpret the information coming into them from the environment. Every organization will face choices as to how it uses the available tools to shape its culture, structure, strategies, and styles to guide it to success.

The chosen paths will profoundly affect the lives of corporate employees, their families and the communities that depend on these organizations. Therefore, consideration of these choices and their potential impact is a critical task of management.

The key in the transformation to the new organization is *fit*. Fit is the appropriateness of one aspect of the enterprise within the context of the rest of the enterprise. For example, one might ask if the means used by people in the organization are suitable to reach its goals. Recently there have been a number of management books exhorting leaders to develop more democratic organizations. Some leaders have defined, as a business goal, more democratic management of the company. Imagine the confusion if the leader were to then *order* his subordinates to become more democratic. The authoritarian means clearly do not fit the goal being sought. Less dramatic examples abound, particularly with respect to trying to develop more flexible organizations without creating more flexible support systems such as reward schemes. If the means such as reward systems do not concretely profit those who demonstrate increased flexibility, (as when a person who tries a new approach to a problem is punished for this attempt), then the means and goals do not fit.

Another aspect of fit concerns the appropriateness of the relationship between the means used in an organization and the people who must implement the strategies. Many organizations still have very bureaucratic systems in place for decisionmaking. Yet the employees they are hiring now are often prepared, both educationally and psychologically, to make quick decisions using many of the new tools now available. When the employees' attitudes and skills clash with the systems in place, it is clear that such a mismatch is not going to help the organization prosper. The introduction of new office technologies creates the opportunity to change many of the means used within the organization. But only by looking at the people and the goals will the means chosen be appropriate to the overall betterment of the organization.

And, finally, we need to be concerned with the degree of harmony among the people within the organizations. The clash between value systems and attitudes of various members can certainly create conditions which hurt the functioning of the enterprise. Conversely, when people value the same traits in each other and understand the same languages (behavioral as well as spoken), then the seeds for cooperation and productivity are there. In many high performing organizations — particularly new, entreprenurial ones — observers are often struck by the similarities among the workers, such as computer programmers and systems designers building a new computer.

Integration is achieved when all members of the organization recognize the need for, and work together to create, the proper fit. Those charged with designing tools and systems and those charged with selecting, developing, and rewarding the people in the organization, cannot work separately from those charged with determining the goals of the organization. Many of the case examples used in the following chapters will demonstrate the problems that occur when this simple fact is ignored.

The changing environmental demands are causing senior management to see whether the goals that have been pursued in the past are still relevant. In many cases, there must be a realignment of goals to stress the need for flexibility and responsiveness. For example, there have been a number of challenges lately to the idea that oil companies need to be fully integrated to be productive. And in some consulting firms, there is a rethinking of the growth goal as small, very flexible firms begin to win very large projects that formerly went only to large firms. In cases such as these, there must then be a readjustment of the other relationships to ensure that fit is achieved.

This readjustment, however, is not always done. All too often, decisions about the structure and functioning of means such as integrated office systems are made in a vacuum, ignoring the goals of the organization they are meant to serve. An instance would be when an organization acquires a system which centralizes decisionmaking just as the organization's senior management embarks on a reorganization which emphasizes decentralization. The reasons for this are all too understandable. Too often, those charged with implementing the systems are not themselves fully integrated into the organization they serve. When responsibility for office systems is given to a consultant or to a systems group that is not equipped to provide the information needed to make appropriate decisions, then the systems implemented are designed to meet the needs of the implementors, not those affected by the implementation. When this happens, it is not unusual to find that the tools chosen (the means) are not in harmony with the goals of the organization.

Not that these support people are unnecessary. The internal and external consulting expertise will be invaluable to the organization. But the need to ensure that the means fit with the goals imposes a requirement that senior management be actively involved with the process of planning and implementing any integrated office system. Otherwise, it is too easy to find yourself on the receiving end of a standardized rather than a customized solution to your organization's needs. The old joke is that, to a small child with a hammer, everything looks like a nail. Well, to a specialist, most problems look like they require his or her speciality. For example, to a training person, most personnel problems could benefit from a training solution, yet the same problem viewed by a systems person might cause a new office tool to be introduced! It is the wisdom and guidance provided by line management that enables successful companies to channel and benefit from the experience and skill provided by specialists.

The means, such as integrated office systems, must suit the people in the organization. This is the most important part of the readjustment process. As it is *people* that must use the means to meet the goals, their needs and skills must be taken into account. The "new employee" discussed in the last chapter is more fully equipped to deal with the changing environment that is now the norm. These people want and need the independence and autonomy to make decisions and react quickly to the many demands. They need to understand the goals of the organization so that any decisions can be made within the same framework. Those in the organization who are responsible for supporting the employees need to work closely with those involved in new technology implementation so that the skills and needs of employees are used as a basis for the design of systems that can be used to move the organization toward the goals chosen. Through this, fit can be achieved.

Predictions

We do not know exactly how any particular organization will change. Each has different forces acting upon it; each has a culture that tends to channel change in different directions. There are, however, some predictions that can be made about organizations in general. Trends are already becoming clearer and we can make some intelligent guesses about the general changes that will be forced by the new environment and the new employee.

The first obvious trend is that change is with us to stay. There will be no return to the "good old days" or the "good old ways". Therefore, structures that worked in the past cannot be relied upon to work as well in the future. It is not a matter of waiting out the turbulence, turbulence *is* the stability of the future. So our organizations must be structured to be constantly adapting and evolving. Our management must become adept at analyzing trends and taking active steps. There is little time for reaction now.

In concrete terms this translates to an organization and management that is "Lean and Mean". Few will be able to staff at previously accepted levels and still be able to change direction quickly when it is needed. Successful organizations will continue to seek ways to handle more work with fewer people. As wages and benefits have become one of the largest costs of doing business, and as reducing existing employment levels becomes increasingly more difficult and expensive, this is a natural outcome.

This does not, however, mean that the need for staff will necessarily decrease in a particular organization. It is true that some of the new technologies allow each person to do more than she or he could in the past. But, at the same time, they allow people to do new things and most organizations want these new things done. For example, many organizations do not currently have sufficient expertise to monitor trends and movement in the marketplace to be able to plan for needed changes. Some new office technologies allow this monitoring function to be handled more capably. Consider how certain supermarket chains monitor the sale of specific items on a moment-by-moment basis to see the effect of pricing and location decisions. Using this information they can more accurately predict sales volumes and adjust inventories appropriately to contain costs without losing sales due to stock-outs. These chains have a cost advantage over their competitors despite the need for market analysts to evaluate the new information available.

In addition, organizations must not staff at so low a level that they are unable to afford the "slack" time needed for reflection and reassessment. As is obvious from the preceeding chapter, those organizations that can move quickly and adapt to new demands will be most successful. If everyone in a particular enterprise is working fulltime on today's job, then no one is paying attention to the new information which indicates the need to adapt. So the need for people who can think as well as do is still with us.

Therefore, it is possible to have an increased need for people as a result of introducing integrated office systems. This is rarely a problem, because the same technology that creates this need also makes the organization more competitive, because it supports the introduction of innovative activities. In other words, the new activities are justified by the fact that they pay for themselves over time.

A corollary to the "Lean and Mean" prediction is that most organizations will delay hiring new people when workloads increase. This results, of course, in an increased workload for the current staff. While acceptable for the short run, most organizations will seek to reduce the burden in two ways. One way is to turn to integrated office systems to increase the productivity of workers. A second, more immediate one is to reduce the burden on permanent employees by increasing the use of contract labor.

It will be more common to hire people for specified periods of time (for example, on yearly contracts) to perform specific tasks or projects. This will happen at all levels of the organization. The reliance on consultants and other professionals will also increase.

This change in the basic employment relationship is consistent with the orientation of the new worker. The individual's desire to be independent and to engage in lifelong learning has historically not been met in large organizations. We are finding that there is an upsurge in the drive to be entreprenurial or to work only for small companies.

Also, in the recent past, we have witnessed the layoff of many long-term employees of large organizations. For many people this was the first time that they realized that company loyalty was not a two-way street anymore. Though much is made in the popular press of the Japanese concept of "lifelong employment" (limited though its application may be), in fact many North American companies had, for many years, been following an implicit strategy of encouraging employment for life. In many large oil companies, for example, it was very common to find employees who had joined the company after finishing high school or university and never worked for anyone else. This was very common in retail organizations as well. In the 1981-83 recession, people with twenty and thirty years of work service were laid off or given early retirement. The experience was shattering not only for those directly affected, but also for all other organizational members. It is doubtful than many organizations could find employees willing to make a "lifelong" commitment or believe it possible anymore.

What has begun to emerge is a trend that will, no doubt, grow in importance and scope. Networks of organizations that constantly use one anothers' skills are developing. For example, many large organizations will use small companies to provide services in such areas as public relations, financial advice, legal work, engineering studies and facilities planning.

This is the beginning of a new organizational relationship which, for successful companies, will not be a transitional form, but rather a new way of working. To maintain themselves as "Lean and Mean", they will protect and nurture the parts of the organization that directly contribute to the production of the final product. Related, but more peripheral activities will be candidates for subcontracting. And this will suit the smaller firms who will be staffed with the innovative, entrepeneurial employees that the large organizations have difficulty attracting anyway. These "consultants" will service various accounts, thus meeting their own needs for variety and growth.

This transition to a new organizational form will create some problems for those who must design and manage these organizations. Large and small will both face challenges that have not been present before. In the later chapter on organization, these challenges will be further explored. For now, it is sufficient that you understand that the organization will be evolving and that this change needs to be anticipated during the implementation process, which is the subject of the next two chapters.

No change is simple; none affects only one part. Because any organization is a complex and constantly moving conglomeration of people, structures, goals and culture(s), all change is complex and the effect of it will be difficult to predict. But the attempt must be made and management of the impact is an essential responsibility of the senior people.

The introduction of any system which, by its very nature, affects all people and departments of the organization (as, by definition, integrated office systems do), cannot be viewed as a benign introduction. It *will* create change. The issues are what kinds will they be, who will control them and who will be monitoring and evaluating the changes to actively manage and guide them. As we will see in the next chapter, with proper preparation, the responsible people within organizations can and must become initiators in managing this change process.

MANAGING THE TRANSITION:
Where Do We Go from Here? How Do We Get There? How Will We Know We've Arrived?

2

Planning for Change

Clearly we are in a time of transition. The changing markets, people and technologies demand we take a new look at how we are organized and at how we operate. Navigating through these turbulent times will test all managers. Although they must be faced, many of the issues relating to business effectiveness are beyond the scope of this book. However the issue of technology in the office well deserves our special attention.

There are three major questions to be answered when looking at organizational effectiveness and, in particular, how technology might help you to become more effective. These questions are the focus of this section of the book. This chapter looks at *Where do we, as an organization, want to be in the future?* In relation to this, we must look at what tradeoffs need to be made and who is the most appropriate to answer this question. The next chapter examines *How do we get from here to there?* This question assumes you can say where you are now, but we will look at how to discover your position if you should need to. The final chapter of this section focuses on the question *How do we know that we got there?*

If the only concern were to get the best technology for the organization, then a technical specialist could be called in. But the true task is to develop the most effective and productive organization possible and the issues involved in this are more complex. The best technology in the world, poorly implemented or inappropriately choosen, will be a disaster. The major issues of organizational effectiveness and productivity are *human resource* and *managerial* issues. Where are we going and how will we get there are questions that cannot be answered by focusing solely on technology.

Leading the Change— Senior Management's Role

Any consideration of new office technology requires very early input from senior management. Regardless of who has initiated the investigation, when it comes time to begin seriously considering technology, senior management must be involved. Of course, they would have been involved from a financial standpoint; they would have been asked to authorize the purchase of equipment and other related expenses. But here we are talking about a very different kind of involvement.

The introduction of new technology is not an end in itself, it is merely a tool to help the organization go somewhere it wants to go. The focus must then be on

- Where are we going?
- What tradeoffs are we willing to make during the journey?
- How are we going to get there? and
- How will we know that we have arrived?

It is only senior management who can answer these questions for the enterprise as a whole. It is up to them to ensure that any changes being made to the organization are consistent with the answers to these and similar policy questions. Once these have been answered, other organization members have the framework for making decisions that are consistent with senior managment's desires and visions.

This framework will be used in defining the standards against which all decisions regarding new technology will be measured. So it is important that the organization, as a whole, has a published and commonly understood set of criteria for what outcomes from the introduction of change are, and are not, acceptable.

The published set of standards will be vital to those with the responsibility for selecting the hardware and software tools chosen to support the organization's quest for enhanced productivity. For there are many kinds of technological tools available and each contributes to supporting or undermining particular organizational values. It is a mistake to think that technology is neutral or "value-free" and that an inadequate implementation is the only cause of dissatisfaction and low productivity. In fact, designed into each product (hardware and software) is the "philosophy" of the designer. This philosphy is based on the assumptions used by the designer about how people work. For example, if a particular software program includes the ability to closely monitor the individual actions of employees and if the program makes this information available to a supervisor but not those being monitored, then the philosophy used in designing the software is from the Scientific Management school that assumes people need to be closely monitored in order to ensure that they perform.

In choosing to purchase one product over another, the organization is supporting the design philosophy of the chosen product. This happens without anyone realizing it because, unfortunately, neither the designer nor the purchaser of the various "wares" have been trained to recognize or articulate the individual philosophies hidden in the technology. If they did, purchasers might better understand the impact of using the "wares" in a particular organizational setting.

So it is that we end up with organizations purchasing equipment that, in philosophy, articulates the view that workers are stupid, lazy and probably dishonest. This is exemplified in software that measures employees on minutiae such as keystrokes per second (with reports to the supervisor as to where each person ranks *every hour*). This may be suitable for an organization which has traditionally acted on the assumption that its employees are stupid, lazy and dishonest, but managers in most of the successful organizations are moving away from these assumptions and finding it profitable to do so. For them to choose software that represents a regression to an earlier, now abandoned management style would be a tragedy. Senior management needs to clearly state that the purchase of any equipment or training must be consistent with the organization's philosophy and desired way of doing business.

Also, we see software that demonstrates the assumption that the mind of the systems developer is typical of all users. One such "user-friendly" system required the user to know the Julian date in order to begin using the machine! (For all of those readers who, like most people, have never known or long since forgotten the concept, the Julian date is a numerical way of giving the date, with January 1 being day one and December 31 being day 365 or 366.

How can senior management ensure that its plans for the organization and the philosophy underlying them will be used as the framework for decisionmaking when introducing new technology? The first step is to agree on the values the organization holds and expects to be enhanced by any change that is to be labeled "progress". These might include enhanced opportunity to develop new skills, increased productivity, greater flexibility and new career opportunities. As well, they should define those outcomes which are unacceptable and to be avoided. These might include increased stress levels, reduced job satisfaction, increased efficiency at the expense of effectiveness, and increased turnover and absenteeism.

When this has been done, those responsible for proceeding know what is expected of them. They know what outcomes are acceptable and unacceptable and know that they must collect evaluation data that allows senior management to measure the actual outcomes in these terms.

And they know that they must use a process that is most likely to result in the desired outcomes.

The work involved in making the organization's values public is, in essence, the process of examining and communicating the corporate culture. That is, making explicit "who we (as an organization) are" and "what we (as an organization) value". In defining and communicating these values, senior management conveys these values to the entire organization, in very concrete terms that can be used in decisions regarding the choice of productivity tools and techniques. For the senior management team, this may be the first experience with such a task and it provides them an opportunity to demonstrate the leadership for which they are being paid.

Another task which the senior managers must perform is to provide visible support for the introduction of new technology if it is deemed to be valuable to the organization. They must also develop an understanding of how this introduction will affect the enterprise and the people who work within it.

Visible support can be demonstrated in many ways: membership on an implementation task force, volunteering as a pilot site for initial introduction, and active participation in the communications which take place before and during the introduction phase.

Developing an understanding is equally important. This education involves learning how technology will affect the operation of the organization, how it may alter the way work is done and how it may in the long run alter the products and services being offered. Senior management must gain this insight in order to adequately assess the work being done by those below them.

Senior management and senior union members are key to the success of any implementation. It is through them that the methods of approaching technological introduction will be established. And they will not be able to perform this role if they do not have sufficient information to feel comfortable with the topic. Their support is prerequisite and so their understanding must be enhanced.

Gaining this understanding must begin very early in the planning process and well before the actual introduction of any new technology. Those involved in the introduction of technology require a good understanding of the potential benefits and possible problems, so their first major tasks should involve activities which promote awareness of and skill in dealing with the potential outcomes of their actions. Anyone who will be involved in understanding the potential impacts on the organization must first become familiar with what is possible and available in terms of hardware and software and then must learn what other organizations have experienced to find out what might be suitable for their own organization.

Planning and Implementation

In the old days, that is, prior to the 1980s, "computers" were "installed". Now "systems" are "implemented". It may seem like a trivial point, but the change in jargon represents a new way of viewing the introduction of new technology. According to my dictionary, "install" means "to set up for use" while "implement" means "to . . . ensure actual fulfillment by concrete action."

The main focus of attention has shifted from what is done *to the machine* to what is done *with the people*.

Unfortunately, the change in attitude represented by the change in terms has not been universal. Too many people still view the process of acquiring technology in a very linear fashion. First you conduct a feasibility study, then you go away and design the system, then you make the necessary changes to the physical space, then you implement, then (maybe) you evaluate the results. To these people, implementation is one stage in the process of acquiring a system. As such, it is planned and executed *after* most other activity has taken place. In effect, for them, the implementation is, in fact, still just an installation.

In fact, implementation is *itself* a process rather than one step along a straight path. As you will see in this chapter and those following, it is a complex, circuitous journey of sorts in which you often have to return to square one, building upon your experiences as you go along. Even more important, perhaps, it is a journey whose first step starts when you, or someone in your organization, *begin* to consider how to use some of the new technologies. Thus, implementation is *an integral component of the planning process* that is essential to the final effectiveness of any new systems introduction. In fact, all of the steps in more traditional systems planning (feasibility study, system design, etc.) become steps in a new planning process that builds upon itself just as the implementation phase does.

Here we will consider only the "non-technical" aspects of implementation. The issues of systems testing, data conversion and the like are better handled in books specific to those topics. The point to remember is that

the technical part of the implementation, no matter how well done, is only one aspect of implementation and perhaps not even the most crucial one.

In this chapter we will look at implementation from the initial planning stages and the relationship between technology introduction and other organizational changes that may be desired. The next chapter focuses on the role and actions of the task force that will manage the introduction, and the final chapter in this section discusses how to evaluate the effect of the changes and determine whether the desired benefits were, in fact, achieved and will continue to be achieved.

Implementation Approaches: Two Scenarios

Implementation is no longer merely the natural continuation of the design process. There are particular issues to be met during the actual, hands-on introduction of equipment which will require your focused attention. It is during the activities known collectively as implementation that all the planning, policy setting and philosophizing about "improved effectiveness through productivity and quality of work life enhancements" will be tested. It is during these times that, to the organization, "actions will speak louder than words (or memos!)".

For this reason, the actual beginning of implementation is during the very first stages of office systems consideration. When someone in the organization begins to consider whether integrated office systems would help the organization, he or she, through initial actions, is already laying groundwork that will affect the quality of any subsequent implementation. And key to this is the recognition that the difference between a successful and unsuccessful implementation is ususally the attention paid to the human resource (or non-technical) issues that arise.

Let's consider two different scenarios. In the first, a person we'll call Ms. Taylor investigates the opportunities presented by office automation. She assesses how much time could be saved by using computer technology to do jobs faster, and to reduce quality problems and increase the amount of work that could be handled by the current staff. As the organizational computer expert, Ms. Taylor does a fine job of analyzing how the organization is currently working and how to make it more efficient and then presents a reasonable business case. Permission is given to establish a pilot project and evaluate the extent to which projected benefits are actually experienced. At this point, Ms. Taylor chooses a pilot group and asks them to involve themselves in the 'experiment'. Work then begins on how to automate current work functions and prepare for the introduction of technology.

This is a fairly typical scenario in business today. It appears, on the surface, to be a rational approach and all our Ms. Taylors are surprised to discover that it does not work very well. To understand why, imagine you are the manager of the group approached for the pilot. You have just been told, by a *staff* person, no less, that you are not running your department as well as you could. That message is implicit in the decision to use your group to demonstate that there are opportunities to improve productivity. How does that make you feel? As well, your people are being asked to participate in an experiment which may well have more negative than positive consequences for them.

Over and over again we find that the pilot does not go well, expected benefits are not experienced and there may even be a *reduction* in productivity. After all, 100 percent turnover in less than a year, as some have experienced, guarantees a reduction in productivity. Or we may find that, efficiency (doing a task more quickly or cheaply) is improved but effectiveness (doing the *right* task efficiently) is not, because the purpose or usefulness of the task automated was never questioned.

In the second scenario, an organization's pioneer, perhaps again from the systems group, whom we'll call Mr. Bridger, has a question. He asks, How must we operate in the future and what role might the new office technologies play? He ensures that senior management understands the far-reaching impact of introducing technological change and gets approval for the establishment of a task force to begin evaluating the opportunities. This task force is made up of representatives from all levels and functions in the company who could conceivably be affected by the decisions made.

In this case, Mr. Bridger has not assumed that his knowledge is sufficient for the analysis and has introduced the concept of participation at the most important stage; that is, before decisions have been made. If, after analysis of jobs and technology, a pilot project seems the way to proceed, participation at this early stage will create an environment within which implementation goes much more smoothly and the use of technology brings the results expected.

In addition, the task force may recommend changes that have little to do with technology — such as the elimination of tasks that are found to have lost their usefulness and the redesign of functions and designs — and these often *further* contribute to the enhancement experienced. In many cases, these non-computer related changes would not have been identified without the involvement of many people early in the exploration process.

In fact, in some cases, the decision may be *not* to automate, with the change in work methods and elimination of unnecessary tasks seen as sufficient and the equipment is not justified at this time. This decision will rarely be reached by an individual, such as Ms. Taylor, looking at the organization from a perspective of "how can I put technology to work in this organization?" Since the wrong question is being asked, it is no wonder that the solution (new technology) is already known, and all that is required is to find the right application. The idea that there may be no right application or that the right application will benefit from the introduction of other changes as well is not even entertained.

What if We've Already Started?

Of course, sometimes decisions about technology acquisition and systems design have already been made and now you are faced with an impending installation which you would like to convert to an implementation. In fact, this is more often the case than not these days. While, ideally, you would like to begin the whole process over again, you wonder if there is anything that can be done to help avoid the problems that come from using traditional systems installations approaches in the introduction of office technology to non-systems people.

In this instance, you will want to compare your own experience to that discussed in this book. Using your knowledge of your organization and recognizing those aspects of the implementation process which have been done appropriately already (we do, you know, often do the "right" or most effective thing without necessarily knowing that it is part of a "new" approach), you can then be in a better position to identify, plan for, and perhaps lessen the effects of the most likely problem areas.

Understanding and Predicting Organizational Effects

A key factor in the successful introduction of new technology is knowing just what the effects of it may be and understanding that both the negative and positive effects can be managed *if properly planned for*. One basic rule is that

during the introduction of integrated office systems, any organizational system that is not currently working well will be highlighted and the problems caused by the non-functioning system will be blamed on the new technology.

This effect has been seen in case after case. For example, in an organization that does not have an effective performance appraisal system, the increased difficulty experienced in evaluating performance on computer-based systems will be blamed on the system. This is because the evaluator has fewer indications as to what, exactly, the person is doing and is less able to see work in progress. Management gets frustrated with the problems of identifying causes of poor work and with its inability to reward or reprimand based on actual examples. In reality, if the appraisal system had been based on outcomes and effectiveness measures, the managers would still be able to judge how a person was doing regardless of any change in tools used. So the problem is in the appraisal system, but the office system will be scapegoated.

In other organizations, the reward system is not a flexible one and may be based on criteria that are unrelated to performance. When integrated office systems are introduced, the new jobs which emerge and the new skills which users acquire are inconsistently rewarded and dissatisfaction results. For example, when word processing was introduced, one company decided that the typists had an easier job and so their wage scale was reduced. In the same situation, a similar company decided that typists working with computer-based technology were doing a more sophisticated task and so were entitled to more money. In neither case was there an attempt to objectively rate the factors that had changed in the work situation and to reward accordingly. In both companies there was dissatisfaction — in the first among the word processing operators themselves, and in the second among co-workers who were not trained on the equipment. In both cases, the technology, not the reward system, was initially cited as the problem.

An inappropriate reward system can destroy any hope of effective implementation. As we will see in coming chapters, the use of new computer-based systems can lead to large-scale changes in the nature of work and tasks at all levels of the organization. To avoid a massive restructuring of the reward system, the organization may be tempted to use old classifications and titles and to base pay on these. While understandable because redesigning a reward system is no small matter, the temptation should be resisted if the current reward system will clearly hamper efforts to improve effectiveness and productivity.

Even if the reward system is fine for dealing with changes to existing jobs or totally new jobs, there may be a push to define a measurable component of the job and to reward for that one component (as in numbers of credit checks processed or number of keystrokes per hour). This piecework payment scheme is rarely appropriate for office jobs and usually undermines the effectiveness of the system.

In one government setting, a new consumer service was initiated in which taxpayers could call in with questions and get immediate tax advice. Those dealing with the taxpayers used computer terminals to find the relevant tax laws and helped the callers understand how their tax situation might be dealt with by the tax department. Because the job involved giving information over the telephones, the jobs were compared to other similar *looking* jobs such as information operators at the phone company and reservation clerks at airlines. Based on this, performance was judged on handling a certain number of calls in a specified time period. The result should have been predictable — callers with difficult problems, or who had difficulty in making their problems understood, received inadequate service. In fact, some people with stutters or difficult accents would find themselves disconnected. The workers felt terrible about this behavior, but knew that their pay and promotions would be negatively affected if they did not "meet the standards".

In each case, the problem is not with the equipment; rather, it is in the attempt to apply an inadequate reward system to a large-scale change in the organization. From these examples we have learned that

the first important task in preparing for technology is to fully understand the changes that are coming and anticipate which parts of the organization are most and least likely to handle these changes well.

It is possible to plan for these changes and to predict the outcomes from various approaches taken. The introduction of new office technology will affect Human Resource systems (such as the performance appraisal and reward systems) very significantly, but you can call on people with skills in predicting how employees will behave when certain things are changed. The people with these skills may be in the Human Resources Department (if you have one), may be certain line managers, or may be found in particularly broadly-trained Systems personnel. Regardless of where you have to go to find the skills, you will find that the planning process is strengthened by the addition of such a person to your planning team.

Summary

Managing the transition is not an easy process. It requires that you pay attention to many variables at once and that you are able to predict possible outcomes of courses taken. It requires the input of many people from different disciplines to ensure that all bases are covered. To coordinate this transition process, a task force is frequently used and the next chapter explores, in depth, what this task force would do.

Fundamental to managing the transition is the recognition, by all involved, that consideration of human resource issues is crucial to success. In this chapter we looked at how to build this consideration into the preliminary steps and shared some insights into the processes that can be used to accomplish this. Now let's look at how to get from here to there.

The Tasks of the Task Force

Each organization approaches change differently. Yet there are some approaches that seem to work better than others, at least in this era, given the new employee, management style, and economic requirements that we have looked at. One approach that has proven successful for many companies is to establish a multi-disciplinary task force to deal with all aspects of the change.

Nowhere has this worked better than with respect to the introduction of new office technology. People who represent the various functions and levels in the organization work together to guide the transition and help ensure that benefits are attained at minimal financial and psychic cost to the enterprise and its members.

The purpose of the task force is to answer the question "How do we get from here to there?" Previous to this, the question 'Where are we going?' will have been addressed in one form or another as we discussed in the previous chapter. Major tasks of the task force are planning for change, implementing change, evaluating the effects of change and, most importantly, communicating with the rest of the organization throughout the planning and implementation process.

Exactly when this task force is established varies depending on how the organization has come to look at new technology. For some, the task force may be struck by a senior management that has attained the level of understanding discussed in the last chapter. For others, there may be a cycle in which one or a few people begin looking into the possibility of using the new technologies, then spend time educating senior management which in turn establishes the task force, or finally, perhaps the task force is established and then finds that it needs to educate senior management in order to get from it the guidance and support the task force needs to carry on.

This task force should include representatives of senior management, human resources, information services, telecommunications (if a separate function), administration, facilities planning, finance, the union and line operations. The members would represent the various levels (worker, supervisory and managerial) in the organization as well as the various departments or functions.

In many small and medium size companies, several of these functions will be represented in one person. This, of course, makes life considerably easier, because it makes the task force smaller and easier to handle. Care must be taken to have representatives from all interest groups that have either some influence over the ultimate success of the implementation or a stake in its outcome.

For the larger organization, it may seem unwieldy to have a group of this size looking into the possibilities of integrated office systems and, if appropriate, implementing them. But experience has shown that

it saves time and effort to include all of the affected functions very early in the process.

All of these functions will be affected by any technology brought in and all the people in these functions will ultimately need to understand and accept the changes that occur. In the end, their support will depend on the degree to which their interests and needs were properly understood and communicated during the analysis and design phases. Also, they are more likely to understand the process when their representatives on the task force communicate back to them throughout the duration of the implementation process.

Information Comes in Many Guises

Communications will, in fact, be one of the most vital functions performed by this task force. Rumors and misinformation circulate very quickly in every organization and it is important that correct information — what is going on, what has and has not been decided, what policies are in effect, what decisions are upcoming, etc. — is made available to every member of the organization. You will find that the office grapevine is a very potent force and shouldn't hesitate to use it as a conduit for correct information about what is happening. Some information will be traveling around the company; you might as well help it to be accurate.

It will be impossible to involve all people in every decision and, in fact, there will be many decisions on which certain individuals will want no input. But if people understand what is happening and how they can have input on matters most critical to them individually (either directly or through their representatives), then they will feel involved to a personally satisfying degree.

One of the most important things to communicate is the corporate philosophy and decision framework discussed in the last chapter. This framework is made concrete by the policies established by senior management. The communication of these policies enhances the ability of the entire organization to make decisions which are consonant with its stated aims. For, as we are just starting to recognize, each employee is constantly making decisions which influence the productivity, product quality and the public perception of the company. But so often these decisions are based on what the employee "thinks" the organization wants. There is little opportunity to actually test this perception. It is tough to be a good team player when you are not sure what the team goals are or which sacrifices are considered the right ones.

As the world moves increasingly faster and employees are being called upon to react even more quickly to demands, it is imperative that all members of the enterprise, up to and including senior management, share a common decision framework. The introduction of new office technology allows for greatly enhanced decisionmaking on the part of individuals and it is the responsibility of senior management to ensure the accelerated speed of reaction is working *for* rather than *against* the best interests of the company.

Task One: Discovering Where We Are Now

The first task of planning for moving from here to there is to be sure everyone knows where 'here' is. Therefore, the implementation process itself, which the task force will manage and communicate, initially involves analyzing organizational needs and capabilities with respect to discovering where the organization is now and in what ways the new technologies could help. This is quite different from the "feasibility study" of old. The feasibility study was (and occasionally, still is) focused on where technology might be used. It rarely went beyond the consideration of which tools would be cost-efficient. The organizational analysis involved here considers the appropriateness of tools only in the later stages of a much more thorough look at all facets of organizational effectiveness.

This is a huge task, but when done correctly proves well worth the effort. In the process, many ways to improve organizational performance, enhance job opportunities for personnel, and create structures within the organization that help increase flexibility will be discovered. Some of these will be immediately implemented as they will not require any new technologies; many of them will have to await the integration of existing and new technologies.

One of the largest equipment vendors used to provide such an analysis to its clients in the belief that many of the organizational problems need to be resolved to ensure a smooth technology introduction. Its study would include recommendations on manual systems, organizational structure and even job design. Some savvy customers learned that if all the recommended "pre-installation requirements" were dealt with, productivity was improved to such an extent that the technology was no longer required! Needless to say, this vendor study is no longer available.

There are many things to be considered in answering the question of where we are now:

- existing organizational structures, policies and operations and how well they are functioning and what changes would be desirable,
- current physical space and furnishings and what can or should be changed,
- current product and/or service lines and how these will need to change to meet changing market demands,
- current personnel and skill availabilities and how these are and should be changing, and
- current and future technologies available to the organization.

You can see that the task force is necessary in the larger organization because no one person could provide the many perspectives required. And, as all parts of the organization are interrelated, with a change in one causing a change in others, the analysis requires that all those on the task force spend a lot of time integrating the various pieces of the jigsaw puzzle to arrive at an understanding of the complete picture.

It is quite likely that the task force will divide into smaller groups to do much of the data gathering necessary. But two cautions are in order. First, use participation on the task force as both an education and developmental vehicle for the members of the group. They will be required to give a lot of time and energy to the process, so they deserve to come away with increased skills that are of use to the organization and themselves. As well, those with less specialized skills will bring an important, generalist perspective to the analysis being done. For example, members of the group doing the analysis of the technologies could include not only representatives from Information Services and Telecommunications, but also perhaps from line operations and Human Resources. These representatives will bring important perspectives to the data gathering and also will be able to assist in translating the findings to other task force members and to the general organization later.

Second, make sure that the smaller groups are used for data gathering and preliminary analysis only. Their findings and tentative recommendations must be seen as input to the entire group, which must have responsibility for the final analysis and all decisions.

These two precautions ensure that any final decisions have been fully analyzed from the total organizational context and are not dominated by staff experts who may not understand their impact on other functions. Too many organizations have arrived at the implementation stage of integrated office systems only to discover that important and expensive factors have been overlooked or discounted.

In an extreme case, one organization discovered that the cost-benefit analysis had omitted training and that, in dollars and person-hours, they had to spend as much on training as they did on the total (hardware and software) system. Full implementation took twice as long as expected, frustrations were widespread, and the system probably never would have been approved if the full costs had been known. Needless to say, there was no representation from Human Resources in the decisionmaking process.

The actual tasks of the various task groups need to be agreed upon by the task force as a whole and frequent reporting back should take place. Within the task force, as well, the communications that will be given to the entire organization need to be outlined and responsibility for issuing them agreed upon.

Each of the task groups will be looking, from their varying perspectives, at the same set of issues regarding technology and the organization. In general, these issues are evaluation, developing policies, and pilot planning. Figure 1 shows the various issues to be addressed and the various facets of the enterprise being studied. Depending on the size of the organization and the resources available, these issues will be addressed in greater or lesser detail; each question needs some answer in order that later choices on implementation be made. Each of the issues will be discussed in the following sections.

It may seem odd to put evaluation first. But you can not wait until the end of a process to think about evaluation. The evaluation process (whether the evaluation of the organization or the evaluation of the impact of

ISSUES TO BE ADDRESSED	FACET OF THE ORGANIZATION			
	ORGANIZATION STYLE, STRUCTURES AND METHODS	TOOLS AND TECHNIQUES	ENVIRONMENT AND PHYSICAL DESIGN	
Evaluation: Current Where are we now?	How well are they functioning? How will predicted changes in market or product influence these? What skills are available; which are in short supply? What are the opportunity areas?	What are we currently using? What is available that we should know about?	What have we got now? What known changes are imminent (leases coming up for renewal, major expansions, etc.)?	
Policy Development How do we do things around here?	Key HR Issues Health and Safety Job Security Training etc. Who develops policy - who consults?	How might new techology change the way we work? What assumptions must all tools have in their design?		
Planning for Change How do we manage change?	How do we handle redesign issues? What protection do we offer those involved in experimentation?	Which hardware and software options will we recommend to test? What methods for testing will we use?	What design factors are important to retain? Who is involved in design decisions? What needs to be done to ensure a proper test? What parts of the environment can we change?	

Figure 1   Examples of Questions to be Answered by the Task Force

changes made) is enormously important and all too frequently dealt with as an afterthought. We will look at it in more detail in the next chapter, but here it is important to understand that the evaluation process which is used *during* the original assessment should be the model which the organization would like to adopt for the entire implementation process should the decision to go ahead be made.

The reason for this statement is that each decision made during the life of the task force depends on the information available at that point in time. You can not tighten up the evaluation process as you get closer to the decision to actually spend money and implement office technology. If the inital evaluation is slack, any decisions based on it will be less credible and the task force could find itself unable to make a reasonable case to back up its final recommendations because of unsupportable (or suspect) inital data and analysis.

Too many organizations have gone as far as implementing trial or pilot systems, to "test" feasibility, only to discover upon completion that there is little or no information available on which to base a decision as to the actual feasibility of expanding the use of technology. This is because the initial evaluation of the organization was neglected or shortchanged and so changes in productivity, morale, quality and/or responsiveness could not be properly evaluated for decisionmaking.

There is, also, a second reason for ensuring any initial evaluations are well done. The organization must see, through the data gathering process and the communication of activities and results, that the task force truly evaluated the options and has made recommendations based on good information. If there is a belief that the task force was biased and had a particular answer in mind when it started (for example, that integrated office systems are the way to go), it will more difficult to convince people later that the results are truly appropriate and that the decisions and actions should be supported. Instead, implementation may be slowed by people who feel that those involved are merely "empire builders" and that other, "more appropriate" approaches to organizational enhancement were deliberately avoided because these did not result in computerization (the perceived desired outcome).

The kind of information that will be gathered is that which is necessary for senior management to make decisions and for the rest of the organization to support the decisions made. In each organization and for each task group, the particular information needs will differ. But in general the senior management, who must approve any plan to go forward with implementation, and the majority of the organization, who must support this implementation if it is to succeed, will need a few basic questions answered by the data analysis. These questions include: What, exactly, are the opportunity areas? Why are these the important areas on which to concentrate attention? What alternatives have been considered and rejected and why? What alternatives are recommended? How will the changes suggested affect the way we work? Is anyone's job, health, or security threatened and, if so, what is being done about this? How will we know that we have made the right choices? and, How have we arrived at these answers?

Garbage In, Garbage Out

The decision on what data to collect is very important. Gathering good (that is, useful and valid) information is more dependent on the task force's ability to ask the right questions than on its ability to generate quantities of data. This fact gives rise to the GIGO Principle: Garbage In, Garbage Out.

However, an often overlooked point is that the *process* of data gathering is equally important. It is particularly important to look at this process of data gathering and data evaluation from a human and organizational point of view.

Data will likely be collected in a number of ways from a number of sources. Information can come from an analysis of the paper in the organization (reports, memos, newsletters, previous analyses; inputs such as invoices, receiving slips and checks; and outputs such as payments, letters and annual reports); from interviews with various members of the organization and its environs (suppliers, customers, unions); from observation of activities which take place; and from yet other sources. Some information gathered is quantifiable — such things as actual number of letters typed, time spent on the phone, numbers of checks issued, number of rejects, time spent traveling to internal meetings, and the like. Or it can be more subjective information, such as how people feel about issues such as the quality of work done, how well the organization deals with complaints by customers, how long it takes to make a decision, whether it is a good place to work, whether it is possible to do the work in better ways, and similar issues.

In your particular company, any or all of this information, and maybe much more, will be needed to determine what steps might be taken to improve organizational performance. The important thing is

to have a plan for the data gathering that ensures people are inconvenienced as little as possible and able to participate as much as possible.

In the ideal situation, no person is interviewed more than once during this preliminary data gathering process. Thus, when the various task groups have defined the information they need, an organized and integrated data collection procedure can be developed. This should allow for maximum input from each person while respecting their time pressures and requiring the least amount of time from them.

If there is a need for further interviews based on new information demands, subsequent interviews should avoid any ground previously covered. This method, when used, has several benefits. First, of course, it respects the time of each person and at the same time provides the best use of the time of those doing the data collection. It also requires that the task force be very organized and structured in its approach to the information-gathering process and this requirement for cohesive planning will be useful throughout the implementation process — they might as well develop skills at it now. In addition, this approach communicates to each person interviewed (and through them to the organization as a whole), that the task force is organized, planning conscious, thoughtful and responsible. This subtle communication can demonstrate to organization members that the task force is efficient and effective, an impression which will be very useful when recommendations are made later.

Contrast this approach with that which has been experienced in some organizations. First, many managers are interviewed for their views on how they could be doing their jobs better. (Note the implication that they are functioning at less than their best.) Then, realizing that there is a need for information on the physical dimensions of organizational effectiveness, the same people are polled for their opinions on how they expect their departments to grow, what the space demands will be, how changes in equipment may affect these needs (for example, with respect to filing) and so on. Then there may be observational studies to determine how time is used in the department and the managers are asked to study and comment on how well these time analyses represent what future behaviors may be expected. Each of these approaches to the managers may have been initiated by different people, perhaps even representing different parts of the organization! As you can imagine, by this point the managers are frustrated by the amount of time this *initial* study has taken, the seeming lack of organization in the data collection activities and the lack of communication between interviewers. The managers' later involvement in any further study may be perfunctory and their ability to support the final outcome reduced. In short, they may tell you to go fly a kite when you ask for more interview or questionnaire time.

Once the data has been gathered, it must be analyzed. The analyses must be objective, complete and *comprehensible*. The importance of the last item is not to be underestimated. Any analysis that cannot be readily communicated to the general population is not likely to be supported by those on whom future success depends.

So where are we? Data has been gathered and analyzed. Despite the fact that a lot of ground has been covered in preliminary data gathering and interpretation, there are no concrete outcomes from the task force as yet. Now, the task force will be expected to come forward with recommendations regarding processes, policies, and planning for implementation — if it makes the recommendation to go forward with a pilot project — or a proposal for full implementation.

The Policy Framework— How Do We Do Things Around Here?

The task force will have the results of the various task group analyses regarding the organization's functioning, technological opportunities, and physical space opportunities and constraints. It will examine all this information to gain an overview of the interrelationships between the various concerns and to understand how any changes in one component will influence all the others. While the specific priorities given to issues will be different for each task force, certain human resource issues must be dealt with by any task force in any company. It is this generic set of issues that will be the focus of the rest of this chapter and, for that matter, the latter half of the book.

There are many human resource issues that must be dealt with:

- Job Design
- Health and Safety
- Job Assurance
- Training and Retraining
- Education
- Communication
- Organization Structure
- Reward System
- Performance Appraisal
- Career Pathing

For each issue, there are a number of questions to be answered. These include:

- Who is responsible for developing policy regarding this issue?
- Who will be required to implement this policy?
- Who (or what groups) will need to be consulted before policies and implementation plans are finalized?
- Who (or what groups) should be informed of decisions made and action taken? and
- Who can assist those responsible?

It will likely be that there are a number of instances when the responsible person or group is not on the task force and so a way will need to be developed to engage that person or group in accepting responsibility for the tasks at hand. Working through these questions on each issue helps the task force understand much more fully the human impact on the organization of the introduction of new technology. Communication of the results of this work helps the organization understand what is coming and that there are people truly concerned with the implications.

It is clear that a great deal of thought and work will be needed to gather the information and do the analysis necessary to even begin to answer all these questions. And each implementation task force may find that its particular organization has additional issues concerning human resources that must be managed. These issues will be identified during the initial evaluation of the data.

One organization discovered that a major concern was the issue of "constructive dismissal", the problem faced when the job for which a person was hired is so dramatically changed that he or she can claim that the effect was dismissal, not just job change. Such claims often lead to suits against the company. To avert such suits, this organization undertook to educate its workforce about coming changes, how each might be affected and that acceptance of job changes as a result of organizational change would be necessary for the survival of the company. In avoiding the shock of change, it also avoided the suits that often follow such shocks.

The other analyses being performed on the technological opportunities and the evaluation of the physical space components of the organization will need to be integrated with the organizational facets. Questions listed in the chart, and others important to your particular organization need to be answered. Through these, comprehensive and *comprehensible* policies will be developed to guide the implementation process. There is no question that this is a big part of the task force's efforts. We are not talking here of a minor job!

But it is truly worth the effort. When the task force has worked through

this task, it will have laid the groundwork for a continuing implementation process that will support a *relatively* smooth, well understood and
humane introduction of new technology. It will also be able to fully
understand the costs and benefits of the proposed change and make
recommendations that are sensible and based on a complete analysis of
the situation. To hurry the process and skip this phase is to ensure that
many unsuspected (and unbudgeted) problems will emerge to slow down
and sabotage the introduction of the technology and perhaps create a
situation in which the technology will never provide the benefits expected.
A well-planned, well-documented approach to introduction is *always* a
time saver. The graph in Figure 2, comparing a typical installation and a
managed implementation, shows where the time investment pays off.

Conducting a Pilot Project and Planning for Change

Usually the results of the initial analysis are somewhat ambiguous. It may
appear appropriate to proceed with some form of technology introduction,
but some major questions may remain. Many organizations choose to try
a pilot study or to phase in the introduction over time. This small-scale or
initial project will be a key vehicle for the preparation of the organization
for the acceptance of organization-wide integrated office systems and
will usually clarify the decision regarding full implementation. A great
deal about the attitudes, priorities, true intentions and beliefs of senior
management will be communicated to the employees during this phase
and it would be foolish to ignore the true impact of it. Also, it can be used
to test approaches to the introduction of particular technologies to see if
they are appropriate for your particular organization.

The task force plays a major role in defining the location of the pilot
project and what will be the boundaries or limits of this phase. To do this,
at this point, it will need to augment its members with representatives
from the area selected for the pilot or initial phase if they are not already
well represented on the task force. Time should be set aside to bring these
new members up-to-date on what has happened. If there have been good
organizational communications so far, this will be easy to do. In addition,
time should be spent in helping the new group to work as a full team; the
existence of "old guy — new guy" feelings will only inhibit the workings of
the group. Trying to hurry the process of team integration is fruitless and
ignoring the issue will only frustrate the efforts. There are many people
who have skills in team building; now is a good time to use them.

Despite its name, a pilot project is rarely as it seems. Without dedi-

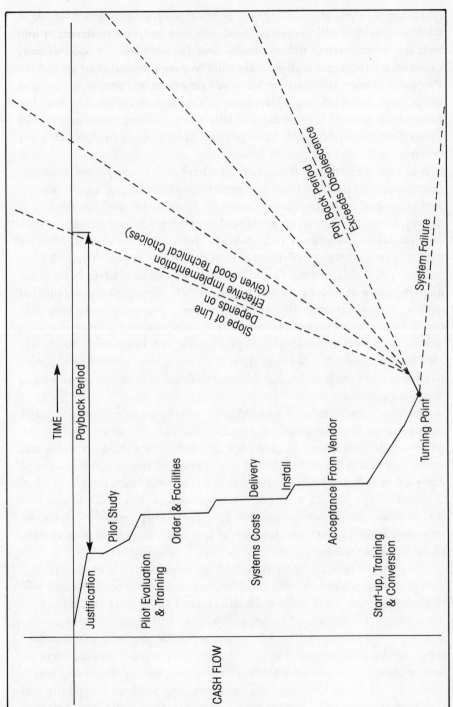

Figure 2   Idealized Cash Flow Curve

cated support for the concept of continuous redesign based on data gathered during the project, most projects become, in fact, mini-installations of predetermined designs that are not open to honest evaluation and redesign. In addition, they are almost impossible to get rid of. Despite evidence that the pilot was a stinging failure, companies can and do go forward with organization-wide implementations that make a farce of the concept of piloting and which are doomed from the start. In this setting, the concept of "pilot project" is analogous to the concept of being a "little bit" pregnant.

A key aspect in the establishment of a true pilot project is the management of expectations within the organization. Here again, a well-chosen, well-managed communications strategy adopted by the task force will prove a valuable force in creating and managing success. Everyone must understand that the pilot is to provide the opportunity to experiment with one or more ways of dealing with the organization's needs for increased productivity and flexibility through the use of technological augmentation of managers and support staff. Remember what we said earlier — the grapevine will be telling a story; you must make sure that the story is based on fact. There must be a commitment to continuous update for all employees which explains what has happened, how it has worked out, and what is being done with situations which have turned out not to meet the standards previously defined or have not provided the benefits expected.

One government agency seemed to be having some difficulty with its pilot project. No one was saying much about it, but when jobs for the particular setting were posted, no one applied. When the staff which was consulting to this area tried to lend its expertise to another one, they were turned down. Word had gotten out that the project "hurt people" and no one wanted any part of it. In fact, things were not that bad and much of the turnover had been planned before the project started (transfers, retirements, etc.), but the absence of communication allowed the rumors to spread unchecked.

The effort to communicate the problems encountered and their resolution produces two important benefits. First, the people learn which policies management truly believes in and intends to support and reinforce. The commitment to stated values and policies will be tested by everyone, and perceived failures to live up to them will take on exaggerated importance because of the natural anxiety which is present during change. Second, the people in the organization begin to recognize, in a concrete way, that the introduction of technology is not without its pitfalls and they begin to rehearse, without even being conscious of the fact, how they will deal with the problems that may be present when their turn at using the technology comes about.

This unconscious rehearsal is an important piece of prework that helps any system-wide implementation progress more smoothly. One of the major failings of most plans for new technology is the failure to plan for times when things are not working out. For example, in one large organization, a new piece of computer-aided design and drafting equipment was ordered. When it arrived, two months late, it failed to work about 50 percent of the time. At first, everyone went on with work as usual. The system failures, while disconcerting, were not too disturbing. But, as more work was transferred to the system and it began to run more reliably, people were more dependent on it to get their jobs done. Now, when it failed, they were unable to use the old ways because too much information was stored in the computer and not available elsewhere. People were left waiting with nothing to do, creating anxiety (How am I going to meet the deadline now?), resentment and anger (If only we could go back to the old way.), and feelings of powerlessness. This is not exactly the emotional state the organization had intended for its employees when the equipment was ordered. The people who were not involved in the project could see the results and became increasingly resistant to the idea of using computer-based technology themselves.

In another, similar, situation the task force and its consultants understood the human problems that can be created by equipment failure — such as feelings of powerlessness, anxiety, and anger which may lead to subtle sabotage and passive resistance — and during the project, created specific tasks that were important and could be accomplished without the use of the technology. Now, when the equipment failed, pilot project members had meaningful tasks on which to work and felt that they were more in control of their work and environment. As well, the planners *planned for* unexpected downtime as a percentage of scheduled work and so the expectations around work production were more realistic.

The difference in approaches is important to both the members of the pilot project and the employees as a group. They can see that equipment failure is a standard part of life and learn, through others' experiences, to be less anxious about it. Also, the organization learns to value contingency planning and flexibility as part of the technology introduction.

Closely related to the importance of communications when planning for a pilot project is the education plan for the organization. There will be specific needs for training, such as user training and the retraining of those whose jobs may have become obsolete or reduced.

In addition, there is a requirement to help all members of the organization learn to deal with the benefits and opportunities provided by new technology. People must be encouraged to try new ideas and new methods, and appropriately rewarded when they do so. Each person will want to know which skills are most important as the organization evolves. How to prepare oneself for the changes which are coming, how each individual can contribute, what is resistance to change and how can it be managed and similar topics will also be of interest to all managers of changing organizations. Later in the book, the training and education issue is dealt with in depth.

The Task Force and the Pilot Project

Some task forces will create a series of task groups at this point in the process to deal with all the details of pilot project planning. Obviously education and communications would be one candidate for a task group. Additionally, groups may be formed around planning for hardware acquisition, software acquisition, organizational restructuring and facilities redesign. Each of these would have a set of discrete tasks to be accomplished in concert with the others. While the last two, organizational restructuring and facilities redesign, are the most obviously related to the human resource issues, none of these groups should be allowed to lose sight of the human and organizational impacts of any recommendations they might make.

The responsibility for dealing with human resource issues resides in each task force member just as it resides in each manager within the enterprise.

Each of the task groups will face the challenge of planning for implementation. Such planning would include such items as:

- the prediction of impact when the pilot is started,
- helping the people in the pilot area plan ways to manage or eliminate any potential negative impact predicted,
- planning the time frame and responsibilities for the change,
- creating an accepting climate among the members of the pilot project itself,
- evaluation of actual impacts found, and
- developing suggestions regarding redesign before the organization considers any system-wide implementation.

Productivity
>   Attainment of Corporate Goals/Objectives
>   Improvement in Customer Relations/Service to Public
>   Cost/Benefit Expectations and Attainment

System Performance
>   System Utilization by User and by Feature Used
>   Ease of Use and Responsiveness
>   System Adaptability

Users' Acceptance
>   User Attitudes
>   Ability of the System to Meet User Needs
>   Support to Decisionmaking
>   Reduction of Inefficiencies
>   User Identification of Desirable System Enhancements

Human/Social Impacts
>   Quality of Working Life Impacts
>   Health/Safety/Stress Effects
>   Incentives/Rewards/Sanctions Changes
>   Privacy/Security Issues
>   Employee Morale/Motivation Changes

Physical Environment
>   Changes Required
>   Suitability of Existing Equipment
>   Substitutability of Alterations
>   Appropriateness

Organizational Impacts
>   Work Methods/Procedures/Policies
>   Training Requirements
>   Labor Relations
>   Effects on Organizational Structures and Relationships
>   Changes in Demographics and Employment Patterns

Figure 3   What Should We Pay Attention To?

In addition, each will need to coordinate with the others so that the collection of data for evaluation and other activities are not in conflict. For example, you would be surprised how many people fail to realize that it doesn't make sense to collect performance data at the same time that the education group is holding information sessions which take the employees away from their tasks and, by definition, is lowering their productivity. That type of problem arises when activities are not seen as interrelated and are therefore not coordinated. The task force continues to be the major force creating an integrated, manageable approach to the pilot study. It should meet regularly to review the work of the groups and to evaluate its own progress as well as to continue planning for the possibility of system-wide implementation.

There is a great deal of specific information that the pilot project or first phase of implementation should provide so that intelligent decisions about the feasibility of further technology acquisition and methods of implementation can be made. Issues of importance have been identified in several pilot projects and include those shown on the chart in Figure 3.

Evaluation of these issues is not an easy task. There is a fair amount of literature and experience on how to judge such items as system performance and user acceptance. Some of the other human resource issues are not as well documented, but it is known that they are essential to successful implementations.

Summary

In this chapter we have looked at the question, How will we get from here to there? We have looked at how to build the human resource consideration into the preliminary study, the pilot and indeed into the structure of the task force itself. The next chapter will explore how to reap the fruits of this good planning from an evaluation that will *reveal* the human and organizational impact of new office technology. As well, we will provide some insights into the processes that can be used to accomplish this. Then we will be able to look at how to move from the pilot phase to organization-wide implementation if the evaluation demonstrates that there will be a positive benefit to the company.

As well, we will see how to include continuous redesign in the original implementation. After all, it is not as though new technology comes into an organization once and for all. What we need to do now is prepare our companies to continuously adapt and modify for their own use any and all emerging tools that enhance the organization's ability to compete in the marketplace. Too often we think of implementation as a point in time; rather, we must remember that it is part of a continuous organizational learning process.

Back to the Drawing Board

Evaluating the Pilot and Organization-Wide Implementation

The separation of the pilot evaluation from the previous implementation work implied by the division of these chapters is, of course, an artificial one. As noted earlier, implementation is an ongoing process covering many activities. The initial analyses performed will, among other things, provide a good deal of information used in the evaluation of the pilot project and must be designed with that in mind. But, to underscore the need for effective evaluation and redesign, we will concentrate on that issue here.

Evaluation of the human and organization effects of introducing new technology will provide two important outcomes. First, it allows for *continuous refinement* during the pilot test. This ensures that negative outcomes are recognized and dealt with at an early time and that the positive can be built upon quickly. As discussed in the earlier chapter, telling the rest of the organization what was learned and what actions were taken helps to set the stage for the next steps.

The second outcome is the final analysis of what went on, what it truly cost, and what the real benefits gained were. This analysis will be the foundation for decisionmaking regarding extension of the process organization-wide. No one can predict with accuracy what these findings will be. Therefore, proper evaluation is mandatory if the decisions made are to be considered credible. Without it, you will not be able to answer the question, How do we know we've arrived?

Tracking Organizational Issues

An important task of the evaluation is to reveal the causes of success and failure in the use of office automation technology to those who must make decisions regarding any future use of the technologies. This understanding will provide a basis for taking necessary corrective or supporting actions to ensure the appropriate use of technology to support the aims of increased productivity and effectiveness. Understanding the causes requires that all contributors to these causes be tracked. Let's look at some of the most important ones.

One important factor to be considered is the effect of demographic variables on the findings. Previous experience has shown that subtle demographic variables can be the cause of acceptance or rejection of technology. By subtle variables, I mean those which are not usually thought of as "demographic" in an organizational setting. These include cultural background, attitudes towards the use of keyboards, and the like. The more usual demographic variables such as age, sex, and level in the organization, while useful in other parts of the analysis, are not very good predictors of acceptance. Collection of data on many variables will assist in understanding how the various factors affect the productivity and effectiveness of the office.

Since it is well known that any change (such as the introduction of technolgy) in one part of an organization will cause shifts in other parts of the organization (such as organization structure or policies), it is important that the results capture the real extent of such adjustments and be assessed to determine which are, in fact, caused by the office automation technology and which are merely coincidental with it. Therefore, care must be taken to track changes taking place within the pilot project site and those such as reorganizations or alterations in union status which affect the whole organization but are not directly caused by the pilot.

Communication patterns are an excellent source of information regarding what is happening within the informal organization and provide valuable insights into the functioning of the overall organization. So the analysis of the form of and changes to the communication patterns within the pilot site will be an important component in the evaluation of the impact of the study on the organization.

The informal patterns of working together are very powerful forces which can resist attempts to change them. Activities which appear unimportant on the surface may be providing rewards that are highly valued by those who engage in them. For example, one introduction of word processing failed because the operators were no longer able to take coffee together! Their informal time for communicating was eliminated and they saw to it that the implementation was a failure. This kind of reaction has been experienced in many organizations which have failed to pay attention to the informal organization when introducing new technology.

The impact of the pilot on leadership and group dynamics also needs to be tracked. All of the new technologies have the capacity to greatly change the ways in which people and groups work together. It is possible to build active working groups from people who are physically separated through the use of telecommunications. There may be fewer face-to-face meetings among people within a department, but more use of task forces involving people from many disciplines with no previous history of working together.

All of this will put new demands on the group members to understand how groups work and how to become productive in a short time. Skills in meeting management, conflict resolution, and leadership will need to be developed by most members in groups using the technology in these innovative ways. Each of these factors — communication, leadership and group dynamics — is part of the informal system that influences organizational effectiveness. Together they have a great impact on the motivation of the people working within the system. In planning for implementation, the possible outcomes of various designs need to be considered and evaluation of *what actually happens* in the informal organization will provide important information for the planning of the organization-wide implementation.

When the individual and small group data is combined and analyzed, it should be possible to see the effects of the pilot on overall work methods and on larger human resource issues such as upgrading or downgrading of job categories, potential for increased mobility as a result of the use of technology, and similar topics. Throughout the study, questions such as the effectiveness of training provided, how training decisions are made and implemented, and the relative usefulness of various approaches to training should be explored. This focus will ensure that it is possible to make recommendations regarding how training contributes to the acceptance and effective use of new office technology.

As has been mentioned earlier, whenever there is a union, it is one of the most important stakeholders in any study. Therefore, it will be mandatory to investigate how the pilot affects the union and its members and representatives, how the union is involved in decisionmaking and what influence this has on the eventual success of the study. Data should be gathered on several levels: behavioral (such as grievances and requests for transfer actually made) and attitudinal (such as how the members perceive their interests to have been served by their union representation). Actual structures in place for ensuring participation and their effectiveness should be examined as well.

The study will be taking place within a context of constant change. It cannot be otherwise; the world will not stand still while the study is underway. Therefore, it is important to track changes that occur in policies, requirements, laws and agreements to understand how these changes have affected the study.

Tracking the Human Impact

Assessment of the human and social impacts of using office automation is a challenging task. The effects can be very wide-ranging and properly evaluating the cause of the impacts requires a competence in several related but differing fields. The methods used to collect and analyze data are very different from those used in more traditional evaluation efforts where system utilization and other "more concrete" impacts are the focus.

Data for the analysis of the human and social impacts should be collected from the pilot project members both directly (through questionnaire and interview) and indirectly (through observation, analysis of existing data and of system use, and review of human resource statistics such as absenteeism, voluntary quits, health complaints and so on). There are a number of questions that need to be answered by the analysis. A brief list will give the flavor of these questions:

- Have individuals and groups found that the introduction of the equipment has significantly altered meaningful components of their jobs?
- In what ways has stress been experienced during the project, what was the source of it, and how has the stress been dealt with?
- How has the reward system (both formal and informal) been a factor in supporting or discouraging the use of the new technology?
- Which kinds of measures or monitoring systems are seen to intrude on personal privacy and how can they be altered to remove the invasion while still providing needed information?
- Is there any information being collected that turns out not to be needed?

This very short list suggesting some of the issues to be dealt with demonstrates the complexity of this area of investigation. It is necessary to gather data that will provide answers on the individual, small group and total organization levels. The data to be gathered includes individual perceptions, attitudes and beliefs — such as feelings about the competence of supervisors and managers in handling the changes and beliefs concerning one's own mental and physical well-being and whether this has changed — and so the data gathering exercise must be carefully and sensitively handled. Again this underscores the importance of participation by the individuals who are affected by the change. If they have control over their own data, you will find that it is more honest and complete because they will know that you are not using it to spy on them.

An Example

Throughout this chapter and the rest of the book, we will be focusing on the human resource issues that demand constant attention during change. Here we will use a case to help us understand the various aspects of evaluation that are being introduced.

This study of the redesign of the administrative support function to increase the effectiveness of the people and to rationalize the use of technology was conducted over the two-year period between 1981 and 1983. Central to this effort was the design of an ongoing evaluation of the impact on people. The study was used both to assist in redesign as needed and to help the government department involved in setting policy regarding future implementations.

The setting is a government department in which services are provided to many field sites. The services are mainly of a financial and assessment nature and many employees are in the office only part of the time to write reports and analyses. Each unit had its own set of support staff: clerks, typists, secretaries and receptionists. Due to the nature of the work cycle, some staff would be very overworked while others had no work because their people were in the field. The overload would vary for each person throughout the year.

Each department was acquiring various forms of technology to assist in managing the workload: word processors, telephone systems, and the like. Because the decisions were made independently, the technologies were not necessarily compatible and people trained on one were not able to switch to another to help out.

Upon analysis, it was seen that organizational benefits could be derived if there were compatibility of equipment and better organization of the support staff so that work loads were more managable and equitable. The support staff of three departments were brought together in one area and the physical, technological and organizational aspects of their work totally rearranged. In effect, a new organization structure was created.

The architects of this new creation were the office administration internal consulting staff supported by the computer consulting staff. Jointly they designed the structure, jobs, reporting relationships and tasks of the new group. Then, because the new group was to be relocated to a new floor, they set up a task force with members of the new group to design the physical layout of their area and select furniture and models of equipment to be purchased.

At this point, the manager of the administration group went to senior management to gain funding for this design on the grounds that it was a "pilot project" which could pave the way for further restructuring throughout the organization. Methods for measuring the impact on productivity of the workers were included in the funding proposal. Funding was granted, but the requirement to assess the "people impact" of the redesign was included.

That requirement initially stymied the consulting group. Back in those days there was little discussion in most organizations of this topic. The journals and magazines were just beginning to point out the need to pay attention to people, but little was known in computing circles about how to do it. They asked: What, exactly, was a "people" impact? How could one know about such things and document them? Other questions of this sort presented themselves. But, gamely, they pressed ahead and engaged me as an outside consultant to measure the impact of what they were doing.

As we know only so well, you often have to make the best of a situation that is far from ideal. Evaluation was begun *after* the changes were in place, so there was no opportunity for any "before" measures on the important human and social issues. To provide qualitative data, comparative measures were used instead. That is, a group was found who was working in a situation similar to that of the group in question before the changes were introduced. This comparative group was given the same questionnaires and logs, so it was possible to gain information as to how the group under consideration may have felt and behaved before the changes.

It is always less satisfactory to use a comparison group rather than true "before and after" data, because the assumption that the two groups are truly comparable is too often a tenuous one. But, when that is all you have, it is better than nothing. In this case, the information generated was quite revealing.

In the redesign effort, the "old-fashioned" approach to job and organizational design had been used: jobs were reduced to their component parts and then supervision was added to ensure that the individual jobs meshed and that work was performed. The new jobs were Administrative Clerk (receptionist, mail clerk, and file clerk), Word Processing Operator, and Administrative Assistant (performing general administrative tasks with no typing or filing duties), Supervisor (one for each category), and Coordinator (to whom the three supervisors reported).

This was in contrast to the earlier design which had only three categories of worker: Clerk (mail, filing, some reception), Clerk-Typist (filing, typing, reception, and general administrative duties), and Secretary (higher level administration, typing, filing, reception and other office duties).

Supervision and coordination had not been specific jobs; rather the work was supervised and coordinated by the persons for whom they were working. The quality of this supervision and coordination varied widely based on the skills and inclinations of the individual managers involved.

There were many reasons for settling on the new design. It would provide more consistent supervision and coordination for the employees. Pooling the use of word processors would allow for the use of technology in a more consistent fashion (in some areas the word processing had been used a good deal, in others, hardly at all). Through increased specialization, productivity gains and cost efficiencies could result. And as a side benefit, it would create two new levels of supervision to which the administrative employees could aspire, thus increasing their career options. On paper it sounded great.

The first evaluation demonstrated that the project group was not producing the gains expected. And there were clear indications that the reasons for this finding were based in the job design and organization design assumptions. In addition, failure to adequately plan for the human resource impacts of the change contributed to the dissatisfaction and reduced results.

To take the job design issues first. The motivating power of the jobs in the pilot group and the "traditional" (unchanged) group was compared and an interesting pattern emerged. Using a questionnaire — in which the higher the score, the more the job is perceived to be a motivating, challenging and interesting by the person holding that job — and other interview and numerical data, we were able to see that the new design has both enhanced and reduced the quality of the jobs. The chart in Figure 4 shows the actual scores.

Technologically Driven Redesign		Traditionally Designed Office	
Administrative Assistant	130	Secretary	110
Word Processing Operator	93	Clerk-Typist	101
Administrative Aide	91	Clerk	103

Figure 4   Job Design Impact

This is not an uncommon finding. When a group has boring, repetitive tasks removed from the job, while at the same time, being allowed to do more interesting tasks, its level of motivation will typically increase. Conversely, when a number of tasks is taken away and the group is required to focus on one specific task all day long, it is not unusual to find the motivating power of the new task is less than that of the previous job.

How does this translate into the experience of real people? Simply, the Administrative Assistants found themselves being used for more administrative and organizing tasks. With the typing and retyping of reports and memos eliminated, their filing now consisted of creating requests for files, not having to find the files themselves. The large increase in the motivating score (from 110 for a traditional Secretary to 130 for the Administrative Assistant) reflects their feeling that they were using more of their intellectual and quasi-management skills and fewer of the clerical skills that they had used before.

On the other hand, the other two groups found themselves severely disadvantaged by the change. For one thing, the clerk-typists were now word processing operators doing word entry but no other typical clerical jobs. And the administrative aides were doing the strictly "low-level" jobs: telephone answering, mail delivery and file maintainence. This is not to say that these jobs are not necessary — the organization could not function if the phones weren't answered and the files weren't maintained — but that these jobs were valued less highly than the administrative and secretarial jobs.

The support staff reported a considerable lowering of satisfaction with their work and an increase in stress felt. This was attributed to several factors. First, the word processing operators were experiencing firsthand the result of unmanaged expectations. The people submitting work to the unit had no idea how the equipment worked and believed that the jobs were now considerably easier to do. So they reduced the care with which they themselves worked, submitting manuscripts written illegibly in pencil and demanding immediate turnaround. Many behaviors that had not been seen when they had secretaries and clerks now appeared: requests for redrafts of minor memos, requirements of letter-perfect first drafts and the sudden need to have every submission considered urgent. Comments from the operators such as "We are expected to produce good work when the input is poor" and "They are asking for too many revisions" were common.

The operators also found themselves in a double-bind. They were not permitted to change anything on the original submission (spelling, grammar, minor editing), yet were seeing their workloads increase dramatically with the increasing requests for revision. All work was funneled through the supervisor and the operators and the people for whom they were working were not in direct contact because it was thought to be distracting for the operators to be interrupted. This made the operators unhappy and prompted comments such as "We don't know the authors — it's not like before — no personal contact" and "We have lost our individual personalities — now we are only a function."

Specialized training for word processing equipment was given only to those designated as word processing operators. Therefore, there could be no switching of jobs and additional support when workloads fluctuated. The same was true for the telephone receptionists. All of these combined to create feelings of increased pressure, reduced independence and variety, and increased dissatisfaction.

When the internal consulting team reviewed and appreciated the significance of the results, redesign work was resumed. A group representing all of the administrative support staff worked closely with the team to redesign the jobs, recommend changes that would decrease the problems uncovered and create conditions for increasing the ability of people to learn each other's jobs.

Some of the recommendations were accepted and some changes occurred. However, the fundamental alteration proposed by the administrative team was to break up the functional units and move the employees adjacent to particular areas of the various departments and to work in teams supporting those areas. Management rejected this outright. Most of the changes which occurred focused on the functional units themselves and involved rather minor changes; no attempt was made to involve the people who were being served by the units even though this had been strongly recommended by the redesign team.

A second evaluation was done several months after the changes were made. This evaluation showed that, in those areas for which the other, less radical changes were made, the scores improved and the respondents reported increased satisfaction. Productivity scores were still not up and interviews showed that the employees had developed ways to frustrate the data gathering methods used to compute these productivity scores.

Additionally, for the first time, concerns were being expressed regarding the health aspects of working with the equipment. Many of the people had worked with VDTs for a year or more, but were now reporting headaches, muscle strain and fears concerning the possibility of radiation hazards. Their concern showed in comments like: "Everyone is concerned about radiation. If it's not OK for pregnant women, then it's not OK for anyone" and "I used to have a lot of energy after a day of typing. With this equipment I'm exhausted at 3 p.m."

Again, attempts were made to correct some of the problem areas identified. But fundamental aspects of the redesign were once more ruled untouchable and so the final evaluation of the project, which took place two years after initial startup, showed very little change in satisfaction. Organizational indicators showed an above-average turnover rate, the emergence of private files (showing a reduced faith in the centralized filing), productivity still below expectations, and a listless, resigned, cynical work group. Additionally, as the consulting group attempted to work with other parts of the organization, they were met with suspicion and outright refusal as a result of the "grapevine news".

Although this case focused on a fairly small unit, the extensive organizational redesign that took place was not unlike that found in other large-scale introductions of technology. It revealed many of the issues that have been raised here about evaluation, planning, and communication and the interrelation among them. The organization was able to use the ongoing evaluation to help in continuous redesign to improve both the productivity and the morale of the employees. But, as is true in so many organizations, there were very clear limits on the willingness of the management to use the information for any redesign which significantly altered the initial design. And, the ongoing evaluation clearly showed the price they paid for this inflexibility.

The problems encountered were not particularly earthshaking. But the resolution (or non-resolution) of these problems had implications for management and there are lessons to be learned in these. The inability to use the information gathered to make meaningful changes in some areas, such as the fundamental design, created an atmosphere of distrust that extended far beyond the pilot project. Word of the problems and dissatisfactions traveled to other parts of the organization, and when the internal consulting group approached other sections to offer help in improving their effectiveness through the use of technology, the approach was rebuffed. In some instances, technology was brought in but the internal consulting group was not used; in others, technology was not brought in.

This organization then, because of this experience and the perception of it in the minds of the employees, has found it difficult to fully approach the issue of office productivity and worker satisfaction. There are avenues that are closed, at least for a while, and time and effort will have to be spent opening them up again.

Many good things were learned during the pilot and many advances made. New supervisory paths were opened to women in the organization that had not previously existed. The time and effort spent paying attention to the physical design of space was rewarded in increased satisfaction and respect for this aspect of the design. Many members of the organization learned a great deal about human resources management and the necessity of understanding the human aspects of technological change. There were some increases in productivity and for some of the employees, morale increased. But these will not be recognized for their worth. Rather, the inability to use the pilot as a true pilot and to understand and accept the need for constant redesign based on evaluation data has inhibited the ability of the organization to build on the successful components of the pilot.

Of course, no single case can illustrate all of the possible impacts on people. Throughout the remainder of the book, this and other examples will be called upon to help you understand how the management of human resource issues can dramatically affect the success of any large organizational change effort.

Implementing Throughout the Organization

By now, you will probably have arrived at two conclusions: paying attention to the "people" impact is an important component in successful evaluation of any pilot project, and, while more complex and less quantifiable than other parts of the evaluation, it *is* possible to evaluate the impact on the human and organizational terms. If the pilot has been deemed a success or at least indicative that the use of new technology will be beneficial to the organization, then the next step is to plan for organization-wide implementation. Surprisingly, this is not as difficult as it might first appear *if* the planning and evaluation of the pilot have been complete, the communications effective and the concept of continuous redesign accepted.

A potential stumbling block in moving to the wider-scale use of technology is presented by the need to manage the expectations of the people. If the pilot has been a rousing success, everyone will want access to the same kinds of support immediately. Everyone will make the case that his or her department is most likely to benefit and should be the next in line. There is a tendency to promise more than can be delivered in the attempt to maintain this energy and enthusiasm.

It will be the responsibility of the task force to control the timing of the introduction of technology and channel the energy. They will need to plan a reasonable implementation schedule and make sure that everyone understands the need for restraint and "making haste slowly". One of the worst problems is to have people trained and waiting for equipment that either is delayed in delivery or is not available in sufficient quantities to meet the demand. The training is wasted as people are frustrated at their inability to use the equipment when they do get it because they have forgotten how. They reject the technology and the idea that they ever thought it could help. Quickly, the positive energy that was present turns to negative energy. They strive to show that their new point of view is the correct one by inappropriate use or underutilization of the equipment when they finally have it.

It is very important not to let this happen. As has been noted many times, it is much more effective if positive, supportive attitudes are formed in the first place. Trying to change negative attitudes is much more difficult and less satisfying than building positive ones.

There is, however, a seductive force to try to "create" demand for the technology. Those in the organization responsible for technology need, of course, to justify their jobs. Often they meet some resistance to organization-wide implementation after pilots. In many cases, the evaluation was not well done or they are seen as too biased to properly judge the atmosphere. So they attempt to create a groundswell of support and demand from the workers themselves in order to demonstrate to the decisionmakers that there is good reason to provide new electronic tools for the people.

All too often, this results in the opposite of the intended results. To stimulate demand, people are shown what the equipment can do and are trained on it. They may be given rather overblown promises as to how much the job will be improved and how easy it is to use. Then, equipment does not arrive on time or is not functioning as it should. The people have to fight for access: scheduling their time on word processors, queing for electronic mail and waiting too long for printouts. Managers get terminals which are supposed to enable them to quickly communicate with their collegues, only to discover that so few of them have the same equipment that memos and phones calls are still needed. A groundswell does indeed appear — to get the "damned stuff out!" It is perceived as a time waster, frustration creator and energy consumer. So much for the guerilla approach to technology implementation.

The more effective approach is to continue the planning and communication method begun earlier. This way the people in the organization are informed of the results of the pilot or pilots, the redesign issues raised, and how these will be dealt with before full-scale implementation. In addition, they will want to know the implementation schedule and when they, personally, can expect to be affected. These and other relevant steps help people maintain realistic expectations and understand the values of the organization.

The planning for system-wide implementation can draw, philosophically, from the concept of "just-in-time", which is in current vogue in manufacturing. The concept is that necessary parts arrive "just-in-time" for assembly so that inventories are minimized. The same concept should be behind the schedule for implementation. Properly orchestrated, people will receive skill training for their new equipment just before the equipment, up and running, is available for them. At the same time that the equipment is available, new furniture, proper electrical outlets and, if necessary, telecommunications links, should all be in place.

They should learn basic skills first, and how to use the same equipment for new tasks just before the equipment is able to support those new uses. For example, it is senseless to teach a manager how to use his or her terminal for electronic mail before there are sufficient number of people hooked into the system to enable the manager to truly change methods of communication. If she or he needs to write memos to some, electronically message others, and phone still others, there is no benefit.

However, electronic mail is only one function. The terminal can still be used by the same manager for time scheduling, report writing, financial analysis and myriad other tasks. Skill training must be suited to the needs of the person and current capabilities of the system. The fact that the implementation of an integrated office system is an evolutionary process is often a revelation to people — they tend to think of it as something that is suddenly *there*.

It should be clear that this "just in time" process requires excellent coordination between those responsible for training, policy planning, systems acquisition, facilities management and telecommunications. In addition, the coordination needs to assume that what can go wrong, will. So, contingency planning and management of disappointment are additional tasks of the task force. All this is a large job, but will pay great dividends to those organizations which make the effort. Such a process of system-wide implementation reflects an evolutionary, iterative redesign approach to change, a philosophical orientation that will help create an organization that is flexible and able to adapt to the changes in the environment that are sure to come.

Who's In Charge Here?

At some point in this process, the task force may be faced with creating a permanent position for one person or group to take responsibility, on an ongoing basis, for the whole area of Integrated Office Systems. In larger organizations, this has been found to be the case, while mid-sized and smaller ones usually do not have the need for a dedicated resource.

Many people have explored the issue of who is best put in charge or where the person should report. In many places, it becomes a power struggle. Those usually singled out as likely candidates are from the computer systems group or from the administration group. In some organizations, there is a telecommunications group and this may also be looked to for candidates.

It is important to have a person who understands fully, from a multidisciplinary perspective, the interrelatedness of the technical and human aspects of integrated office systems. The ability to deal with diverse functions and see problems from various perspectives is more important to success than specific technical skills. The ability to keep senior management involved in managing changes caused by the innovative use of the new technology is another important skill.

There is no consensus yet as to who is best equipped to do the job. In fact, for each organization the relative importance of skills will depend on what is most necessary to support that particular organization's attempts to improve effectiveness. The task force is best positioned to understand this and develop the position requirements if they agree that having one person be in charge would be of use.

This in no way relieves the task force of responsibility for the implementation process. They will have learned a great deal and will be needed to provide guidance and support for the crucial first years.

Summary

In the past two chapters we have covered a lot of ground. It is not really possible to give you a checklist for implementation. But, there are a number of concepts that are crucial to successful system-wide implementation. These can be summarized as:

- Carefully and fully manage the communications process. Recognize that information will flow no matter what — all you can do is help ensure that the most accurate information gets into the system at the earliest possible opportunity.
- Ensure that all decisionmakers understand the ramifications of the introduction of new office technology and will support organizational efforts to manage impacts.
- Create and communicate organizational Human Resource policies *before* problems present themselves.
- Carefully plan and document the pilot projects. Evaluate the results in terms of needed redesign and fully communicate the changes that are being made. Let everyone know that redesign is expected, accepted and supported.
- Make sure that every member of the task force, and others who have decisionmaking power, understand that the "ideal" design (job, organization, systems, or whatever) does not exist, but that there are design principles which can work with the technology to enhance corporate productivity. These design principles are based on the notion that the competitive organization needs to be a flexible, market sensitive and employee-motivating entity.
- A very important organizational factor in achieving the gains expected by new office technology is complete, accurate and timely communication of what is going on.
- The two most important "human" factors in achieving the gains expected by integrated office systems are adequate planning for job design and training, and the implementation of these plans.
- Another important organizational factor in achieving the gains expected by integrated office systems is organizational structure. Creating a structure that is supportive of the organizational goals and which the tools can support is a key task of any implementor.
- Effective coordination of all the aspects of implementation will be a crucial factor in success. Coordination, in addition to the usual meaning, includes such factors as planning for disappointment, "just-in-time" planning and simultaneous communication of similar values from various parts of the organization.

There are many different methods for planning the actual implementation of office systems. Most of these are based on experience and will work to some degree. But that is of little use if the persons implementing, according to whatever method, do not understand the human impact of, and truly value the human input to, the process. Creating a more effective organization takes time, planning, management, energy, participation — and each of these in large quantities.

MANAGING THE
INTEGRATED OFFICE

3

Managing the New Employee

After reading this far, let's assume you are convinced that you will need to predict the human impact of the new systems and that employee participation is a key aspect. Where do you start? In Parts Three and Four, we will explore, in greater detail, where to look for impacts and how various organizations have begun to deal with the issues that arise from the introduction of new technology.

Each person will have different information needs. Some will be more interested in dealing with people from a line management perspective and learning how they can encourage participation and create organizations that support the most desirable behaviors; others will be more interested in exploring specific human resource issues such as training and career planning. This section, Part Three, deals with the more general management issues and the next focuses on more specific human resource managment issues. While all the information is relevant and related, you may want to go directly to the part that concerns you most at this moment, and return to the rest at another time.

The New Management Tasks

We've seen how the world is changing at an increasing rate. New technology allows us to do things, learn things, understand things, and create things that we have never dreamed of. And this is fortunate, because the new economy demands that we become more flexible and responsive if we are to survive in the highly competitive, multinationally based economic environment.

This turbulence will cause profound changes in the ways people work. The impact will not be limited to the lower levels of the organization. It cannot be because the "new employees" at these levels are offering skills and attitudes not previously found and the challenge of managing these people will cause changes throughout the organization.

There is a style, which in this book will be called the new management style, that has proved successful for companies on the leading-edge of these changes. Whether the style is, in fact, new or merely represents an alternative style which has been known for many years, is debatable. The important fact for managers is that this new style is becoming the predominant style of the successful organizations and is a key component to the effective use of the new office equipment. So it is important to understand it.

Given that the technology allows us to do new things in new ways, it is necessary that you create the environment in which these new approaches can be discovered and nurtured. We can not predict ahead of time how we will operate. The integrated office will be the site of continuous discovery regarding how work is organized, performed, and evaluated.

The management style of the future is characterized by the encouragement of innovation rather than the maintainance of the status quo, by participative decisionmaking rather than autocratic order-giving, and by collaboration among, rather than competition between, those within the organization.

Fundamental to this perspective is the recognition that the people within the organization are responsible adults capable of self-regulation when the culture of the company supports this behavior. We will look at each of these characteristics in turn.

A constant theme in exploring the future is the need for flexibility. We all know that the new era will be largely unpredictable. Thus, when demands for change emerge, we must be able to understand and respond quickly to them. The responses chosen will often have to be newly invented, as lessons learned in the past will become increasingly less applicable in the future. The organization as a whole will need to be flexible and innovative. It can achieve this only if the people who make up the organization are, themselves, flexible, innovative and rewarded for demonstrating these characteristics.

It sounds so easy — be flexible and innovative and encourage the same of others. But it is so contrary to the way we and our bureaucracies have always behaved. Even the concepts, stated differently, can be made to seem most undesirable. To be flexible might be seen as "wishy-washy", "pliant", "unable to follow a plan" or, the worst sin of all, "unpredictable".

The innovative is also subject to another description. Consider "visionary", "quixotic", "dreamy", "disrespectful of our past", and "risky".

These are not the terms most people want to see on their performance appraisals.

In the world in which most of us were raised, a premium was placed on stability and tradition. Yes, there was encouragement for research and innovation. But it happened in special places called laboratories, not in the office! In the institutions in which we spent most of our time, the status quo was to be respected. Schools taught the value of listening to your elders, learning to parrot back what they told you, and taking orders. Most companies were structured along the same lines — people "come up through the ranks" and "know how things are done here." Managers planned and gave orders, workers did as they were told.

And it could not be any other way — that was the appropriate culture for that time. Obviously, it was successful. The Western world did very well for a long time using these principles.

But the very success of that orientation created the climate for the evolution which has made that culture obsolete. Economic prosperity allowed many people to go to school longer than in the past and to experience other developmental opportunities which have caused the "new employee" to question the relevance of the old organizational culture for them. In fact, it has always been so — in most instances, the well-educated and well-off rarely expected to tolerate the treatment which they gave others. It is just that now almost everyone wants — and can handle — what was once available only to the few.

The achievements of the industrial economy were based on the production of goods. The most important variable in that success was the cost-efficient production of great quantities of these goods. It is this piece of the structure which has changed most dramatically. In the future, production of goods will still be important, but much of the production will be done in non-Western countries and will employ only a small percentage of North American workers.

The major Western employers of the future will be in a number of businesses. Those that produce a product will probably be managing overseas manufacturing operations. Both manufacturers and service providers will also be in the business of the creation and management of information. Management models based on domestic manufacturing do not fit so well in these industries, where a new crucial deciding factor for success is a climate favoring innovation.

Information and services are not tangible products. To sell such products, the organization must convince consumers that they are getting their money's worth in a product for which proving value is very difficult. Providers must have very good information collection systems that allow them to monitor how much value consumers place on various products. Some of the best monitors are the organization's employees who are on the "front-line" — those who are in day-to-day contact with consumers.

In traditional companies, employees are encouraged to fill out "fact sheets" or other similar market intelligence forms. These then filter up through the various departments, perhaps getting as far as the marketing division if the information contained is not too threatening to those who have previously filtered it. There is little incentive to provide the data. All too often, the orginator never finds out what was done with it and sometimes is even punished if it is unfavorable to someone at a higher level. Change, when it comes, is in response to more traditional market research information and comes slowly, filtering down to the "troops" through memos, training programs, and management meetings.

But, this will not work in the future. Those behaviors which reward the status quo and tie change itself to the forces which protect the status quo will, if tolerated, consign the organization to oblivion. Managers must learn to support change initiated by others and to become more creative and innovative themselves. Consumers are better educated, well-informed and more mobile than in the past. If your people don't respond quickly enough to their needs, be assured that one of your competitors will. It will be less easy to suppress information about the market needs. With the new office technologies, employees will be able to enter market data directly into the system and it will be very difficult to "filter" this data before it is available to many individuals.

How do you support innovation? To do so, you must understand that innovation is, first and foremost, a product of creativity. But it is not synonymous with creativity. A creative person can think of new ideas; an innovative one can select and implement new ideas. The distinction is an important one. We are all creative a great deal of the time; we are rarely innovative.

Many things conspire to stifle innovation. The chief offender is the lack of visible reward for disturbing the status quo. As "babes in the woods" — when new to jobs or situations — we often see changes that, if made, would improve the product or service. This is creativity. When, however, we try to suggest or implement change (that is, when we try to be innovative), we are presented with numerous reasons why the suggestion won't work. If we are persistent, we discover that the forces opposing change are powerful indeed.

As currently structured, organizations are inertia-driven. All change, even change for the better, is difficult to initiate because it requires overcoming the inertia. All organizations are collections of interest groups and these groups have worked out a way of working together which, while perhaps not optimal, at least is understood at some level by all. "That's the way we work around here." or "Don't rock the boat" are common comments. In the face of this, innovation is likely to fail.

To create the climate in which innovation thrives requires a concerted effort by all levels of management. First of all, they must understand and recognize the forces within themselves that block change. It begins at the individual level. Everyone resists change — learning new habits, even positive ones, is not a favorite pastime. Just look at how hard it is to give up smoking or to exercise more, even though we all know how important these efforts are to good health. How much more difficult it is to change our behaviors at work. The positive outcomes are less obvious and there are so many reminders of the old way of doing things. For example, "Why should I send my messages electronically? I like to keep a copy in my file, then I know for sure what went out."

But you can learn to be more open to change. You can learn to recognize the behaviors used to block change — the comments and excuses we use to stop the creative processes in ourselves and others.(For some samples, see Figure 5.) Methods for learning vary for different people. Some may prefer personal learning situations such as those available in individual counseling or the use of one-on-one consulting, which provide feedback on the impact of one's own behavior and ways of making and sustaining desired changes in it. Others may make use of small-group-oriented situations such as creativity seminars, which focus on innovative approaches to management to develop new skills and approaches. And the organization-wide programs such as those found in organizational development projects can provide opportunities for individuals to practice new behaviors and learn to reward new behaviors in others. Remember that you are trying to unlearn habits, if you are serious, you will get some help because we all know that it is difficult to consistently act in new ways. Good intentions ("I promise I won't say 'Yes, but . . .' again") are not sufficient.

In addition to learning to accept change on a personal level, management must work together to remove organizational structures that block creativity and innovation. These structures are powerful and, in some cases, difficult to recognize. For example, at the most profound level, the culture of the organization may be one which stifles creativity. Culture is that framework within which every action in the organization is per-

We've tried that before.
We've never done it before.
I know a fellow who tried that.
We've always done it this way.

It's too radical.
Why change it? It's still working OK.
We did all right without it.
It's too much trouble.

Our place is different.
We lack the authority.
The board won't go for it.
The employees won't buy it.
Admin. will scream.
Customers won't like it.

We don't have the time.
Not enough staff.
It costs too much.
It would run up the overhead.
It isn't in the budget.

We're not ready for that.
Let's put it in writing.
A committee should study it.
We should test it first.
Let's give it more thought.
Shelve it for the time being.

Good thought, but it won't work.

IT CAN'T BE DONE.

Figure 5   Why it Won't Work

formed and given meaning. Culture includes the values, norms, symbols, and traditions of the organization. As such, changing the culture is a large task.

It is easiest to understand the influence of culture when you compare "flexible" organizations with "inflexible" ones. In the former, innovation is supported and rewarded; in the latter, the status quo and stability are valued. The 3M Corporation is known for its ability to foster an innovative atmosphere. It has a constant flow of new products which are the ideas of many employees — not just the R&D group. New divisions are set up to support the products and they are given wide latitude to nurture the innovations. There has been a deliberate policy from the board level on down to create the culture of 3M. Its design has not been left to chance.

On the other hand, for several years the entire North American auto industry was used an an example of inflexibility. The domestic car makers did not heed the indications that their environment was changing and continued to design and market products which did not meet the public need. New products were only offered or supported well after the foreign makers had captured a large share of the market. The culture of most auto companies was traditional, rule-bound, and inclined to cling to methods that had worked in the past but were no longer appropriate. To become flexible, they faced the task of completely redesigning the organization from the level of culture on down. We are already seeing the results of Chrysler's redesign efforts. Much of management's attention and time was spent on redefining what behaviors are appropriate and what work methods will be used. Rewards were given to those who could demonstrate the ability to work within the new framework and the entire organization is now a very different place to work.

One way to discover the culture of the organization is to pay attention to the language used by the people who work there. What positive words are used? Which negative ones? When describing a new idea do words like "dreamer", "not worth the risk" and "payoff too uncertain" get used? When describing the latest mission statement of senior management do people call the company "stodgy" or "solid"; "leading-edge" or do they say it is "marching off into the unknown"? By paying attention to the language of the company, you can see immediately which behaviors will be rewarded or punished (however subtly) in that organization. In this manner, language is used to inform newcomers of the values and norms of the company they have just joined.

One reason for looking at the language is that it gives you clues as to what needs to be changed in the organization to create the culture toward which it wishes to evolve. For example, in one organization, the people who worked on word processing machines were called word processors. But the machines are also called word processors. The implication was that the machines and the people using them were one unit. Indeed, a manager showing a visitor through the office pointed to the general direction of the worker using the machine and said "And there's our word processor." Neither the visitor nor the worker knew if he meant the person or the machine or both. In this organization, the culture was one of valuing machines and not valuing people. People were seen as a bother and an inconvenience. And yet it was a service organization vitally dependent on its people. The attitude that had to change in order to make the most effective use of all resources and bring their costs into line was clear. And in addressing it, one of the first changes management made was to retitle all jobs so that the title described the person, not the machine. In this instance, the word processors became word processor operators — focusing on their contribution, not the machine's. It may seem minor, but it is through such details that culture can begin to be altered, because in changing the words used, you are signaling to others that changes in attitude or behavior are expected.

Fostering Innovation

What kinds of structures support one culture over another? One place to look is the reward system. Does the system reward for short-term results only or does it also have a way of taking into account the long-term implications of actions? This is an important distinction. Innovation is risky — it has costs attached and even the most successful change has a short-term cost in terms of reduced productivity while new habits are being learned. Therefore, a focus on short-term results will invariably support a status-quo orientation.

Does the reward system encourage the taking of risks? If success is guaranteed, there is no risk. So, by definition, risk-taking will occasionally involve failure. If "a failure is a failure is a failure" in the organization — that is, if there is no way to distinguish between reasonable risk-taking that did not prove out and failure brought about by incompetence, then the organization will be one which represses innovation.

At an individual level, it is possible to encourage innovation and creativity even within an organization which does not. Managers have the power to do this. For example, every company seems to have at least one department which is known for developing talent — it is the souce of fresh ideas and management for many other parts of the company. We usually find that the leader of this department protects his or her subordinates from any stifling effects of the organization. This type of manager supports new ideas and lets the person who generated the idea try to make it work. The manager provides numerous developmental opportunities for the people and is not threatened by suggestions for change.

Look for the department in your organization that seems to be the source of much talent and try to find out what that manager is doing. Interestingly, the manager is usually perceived by the rest of the organization to have "plateaued" and may be seen as "too people-oriented". In a status quo-oriented company, the many skills of this manager are disparaged, but she or he is tolerated because it is clear that good people can be recruited from the department. Personally, this manager has often decided that developing talent and innovation is more important than playing the organizational politics needed to get ahead and is content to remain in one position for a period of time.

Innovation, however it is achieved, is crucial to the functioning of leading-edge departments, divisions and companies. The introduction of integrated office systems provides so many marvelous opportunities to change ways of working and relating. There is a synergistic effect in which the support of innovation and creativity helps the discovery of new ways to use technology and the introduction of technology provides the opportunity to try encouraging innovation and creativity. Managers are well advised to look for opportunities to help move their organizations (or their piece of it) into new ways of working that promote effectiveness and productivity.

Participation and Pseudo- participation

The next major characteristic of the new management style is participative decisionmaking. Much is being made now of so-called "Japanese Management", with its characteristic reaching of consensus on decisions before implementing them. In this book, participative decisionmaking has a slightly different meaning.

Participation means that the people affected by a decision have the opportunity to have meaningful input before the decision is made. The key words are "meaningful" and "before". To ask people for their opinion when they do not have sufficient information to give an informed judgment is not participation. To ask people for opinions when they are not sure how those opinions will affect the way they are treated is not participation. And to ask people for their opinion of how to implement an already-made decision is not participation.

Let's explore these a bit. The argument is often made that employees should not be involved in the decision to acquire office technology because they do not understand the area. This argument recognizes that meaningful participation is not possible without informed judgment.

And, indeed, if it were impossible to understand integrated office systems and their impact, the appropriate path would be to have experts select the equipment.

But we all know that this is not the case. It is certainly possible to understand the basics of integrated office systems as they relate to particular jobs. In fact, those selling the technology go out of their way to make sure that the "choosers" understand. What this position is really saying is that the "users" are not worth the same expenditure of effort as the "choosers". A perfectly understandable position from the point of view of the vendor — but let's remember that it is you who must live with the outcome, not the vendor. And whether you, yourself, are a "chooser" or a "user" or both, clearly you will have to live with the "users" and so need to be concerned about their acceptance and ability to work effectively. It is possible to ensure that those who will be asked to participate in the decisions concerning integrated office systems understand enough about their use, impact and potential to make an informed judgment.

Understanding is one factor. Equally important is that the atmosphere or "climate" be appropriate. If the level of trust is not high enough, people being asked to make a choice on a technical issue may feel that picking the "wrong" equipment will reflect badly on them. The definition of "wrong" is itself subjective and could be "not what the boss wants" or "not what we need in the short run". When this is the case, people will hesitate to truly speak their minds and so their participation can only be called tentative, not meaningful.

Finally, most mistakes regarding participation are made when people are asked to participate in implementing decisions that have already been made. The result is "pseudo-participation", which is truly a dreadful position for the people involved. The concept is not immediately obvious, so we will use an example to explain it.

In the case presented in Chapter Six, we saw that in one government agency, the systems consulting group wanted to try a demonstration pilot project to explore the benefits to be gained by using new office technologies. After some analysis, the manager of the internal consulting group presented a proposal to senior management and permission to go ahead was granted. One justification was that, through evening out the workloads and redesigning the organization, the people would be able to handle the growing workload without an increase in staff.

While giving permission for the project, senior management required that information on the "people impact" of the project be gathered. The consulting group understood that people are more likely to support implementations which they have a hand in designing, so they began a series of meetings to involve those who would be affected by the project.

By this time, the decisions regarding which new technologies would be used, which people would be involved, and the design of the project and jobs within it had already been made. Users were to have input on the choice of equipment manufacturer, and furniture.

Imagine the position the users found themselves in. They had had no input into the task analysis, so they were to select equipment without having input as to whether the tasks themselves were appropriate to the accomplishment of the job required or whether there would be better, less expensive ways to accomplish the desired outcome. In order to participate in any decisionmaking, they had to agree to the design already made. Refusal to participate would be taken by management as a lack of interest or concern over changes being made. What a bind for them!

This classic double-bind situation is not uncommon. Well-intentioned managers frequently ask for "participation" when the results of such participation may harm the participants. If a person refuses to be coopted by the manager, then that person is seen as a "Luddite" — one who resists technology. But, in many situations, if the person cooperates, she or he may be increasing the probability of unemployment or underemployment. It is this no-win situation which could be called "pseudo-participation". To be truly participative, the manager must be willing to consider all alternatives, including the alternative of doing nothing, and must not have already made some of the decisions which have such far-reaching consequences. Said another way, the area of discretion for those participating must be sufficiently large to justify their involvement.

Participative decisionmaking does not just arrive one day. The manager who uses this style of managment must work at creating the climate of trust which is necessary. No manager will feel comfortable sharing plans and goals with his or her employees if mutual trust does not already exist. And employees will not truly participate if they do not believe that such participation is based on a shared understanding of the costs and benefits for all affected.

It is possible for an organization to consciously create an environment in which participative decision-making flourishes. First, obviously, senior management must themselves practice it with their own subordinates. And they must visibly reward others for doing the same. This means sharing information that can be used before decisions are made: information on goals, strategic directions and criteria against which success will be measured.

Working with the senior managment, the Human Resources Department plays a key role in creating this environment. Designing reward systems, creating education programs that help people change their behaviors, and providing individual counseling for managers seeking to encourage participative decisionmaking are all tasks which fall naturally within the boundary of the HR Department. In addition, recruitment of those who are sympathetic with this management style is an important task.

As with innovation, however, ultimately it is the individual manager who creates the environment which fosters participative decisionmaking. Managers have many opportunities for and means of rewarding or rebuking any employee. Job assignments, public comments of a positive or negative nature, and performance ratings are only a few of the tools available. The creation of trust falls ultimately on the manager. Of course, it is not a one-way street. But as the more powerful member of the working team, the onus is on the manager.

Cooperative Relationships Hold the Key

When we look at organizations that foster the atmosphere of innovation and participative decisionmaking, we find that the relationships between people can be characterized as "collegial". This is not an accident. Collaboration and collegiality — people working together as equals — are key components of the new organization.

Collaboration emerges when everyone involved understands that it is possible to make decisions and manage events so that all gain. In contrast, the internally competitive organization is characterized by a "we-they" feeling. Competition, of course, is the behavior that is most useful when there is a win-lose situation; that is, when there seems to be no way to rearrange events so that there is no loser.

For example, when one manufacturer looked at ways to make its bids more competitive, one avenue identified was to reduce its engineering and drafting costs. No particular way of reducing them was selected. Instead, engineers and draftsmen were asked to help explore the problem. The drafting union and its members saw that the introduction of new technology might contribute to the reduction of costs. But they thought that the only way to make this happen was to eliminate positions and focused on this "lose" aspect as the only likely outcome. Therefore, they opposed any use of new technology.

However, when representatives of all interested (and potentially affected) parties explored every option, they agreed that a computerized drafting system was an ideal way to proceed. What caused the change? Of course, there were many influences. But one of the most important was the elimination of the competitive stance through the identification of tasks, methods, jobs, systems, and the like which, if adopted, would create more interesting, more challenging jobs for both the engineers and the draftsmen who would be using the system. At the same time, this change allowed the organization to win more bids and keep its employees working. All of this was possible while still meeting the company's need for cost reduction in the design of their product and the union's need to protect its members.

In other words, the people involved moved from a win-lose position to a win-win position. Simultaneously there developed a new respect for the skills of each of the groups and a spirit of collaboration on a joint problem. Of course, there were risks involved; but the increased understanding of and respect for each other's position helped to make the risk more acceptable.

Collaboration and collegiality evolve together. When there is mutual respect for the contribution each person makes to an organization and when all can approach problems and opportunities from the perspective of "How can we make this a win-win situation?", then people treat each other as members of the same team. This team spirit is really what collegiality is. It implies that power can be distributed among members of the team, so each can influence decisions under consideration.

Collegiality is not the same as democracy. The ability to influence is different from having an equal vote. The opportunity to have meaningful input is not the same as having veto power. It is important to keep these distinctions in mind. Too often, the new management style is criticized as being an abdication of responsibility. While it does represent a sharing of decisionmaking (thus increasing, to some degree, the democratic nature of the organization), at all times, someone is responsible for the outcomes of decisions. In fact, there are *more* people who feel responsible for ensuring the attainment of the goals, objectives, and plans which they helped develop.

The manager has a large role to play in providing the environment in which collaboration and collegiality are found. Before win-win situations can be created, there must be the opportunity to learn about the contribution each member makes to the functioning of the work group (be it department, division or otherwise). Then, the manager must foster the climate which allows these opportunities to be acted upon.

Of course, for organizational success in the Information Society, the entire organization must learn to encourage collaboration and collegiality. As with innovation and participation, senior management and the Human Resources Department must play their part in creating and maintaining this environment. All the systems and structures within the organization need to be reviewed to see whether they contribute to the support of the desired new behaviors. One key contributor is the reward system, which should be carefully examined. If rewards are given on the basis of longevity within the organization and on short-term results, then it is likely that the reward system will need to be revamped.

The Role of the Individual Employee

Early in this chapter, three characteristics for the new management style were given. These were support for innovation, trust in participative decisionmaking, and the encouragement of collaboration and collegiality. Each of these has been discussed. But, as mentioned earlier, basic to the attainment of these is the assumption that the people involved are competent adults who can constructively contribute to the attainment of organizational effectiveness when given the opportunity.

Constructive contribution means many things. For example, it means acting responsibly when given tasks to perform. It means having an internal regulation system so that external monitoring is not needed. And it means understanding and accepting the relation between individual actions and group or organizational outcomes.

There are some who would say that employees cannot be given the opportunities because they would not act responsibly. In some few cases, such a view would be right. But for the vast majority, irresponsible behavior of the past can, to a large extent, be attributed to an expectation of irresponsibility and the creation of a situation which supports irresponsible behavior.

Such a statement cannot go unsupported; let's look at some examples. What do people use as examples of irresponsible behavior? In regard to integrated office, many point to known instances of sabotage to new systems.

One common type of sabotage is the deliberate entry of incorrect information into the system. Take one reported case of a hospital, where a clerk responded to the introduction of a new system by falsifying demographic data on patients. The falsification was fairly blatant — patients listed as "newborns" had spouses and children. This information of course had an impact throughout the system. Billing, patient records, schedules, and trust in the system itself were all affected. Most importantly, care given to patients depended on test results that were based on patient characteristics. For instance, when the computer "saw" that a patient was an infant, it indicated whether test results were normal or not in relation to that information. If, in fact, the patient was an adult, a different set of normal levels would have been used. Physicians could have used the computer output to give the wrong instructions for care.

In this situation, the changeover to the new system had been cut very short, parallel functioning of the old and new system was not done, and the clerks were all ill-trained and not sure that their jobs were permanent. They had not been involved in the implementation, let alone in the decision to implement. Management had not gained the trust of the employees and had not created a feeling of joint responsibility for dealing with problems. The workload had increased enormously, but there were no funds for extra help. One person was unable to cope and her acts of sabotage were an act of protest and even a cry for help.

Another common form of sabotage is passive resistance. It is possible to appear to be complying, while at the same time be doing all in your power to slow down and thus foil the implementation. Managers on electronic mail systems often exhibit this behavior. They request training, but then have to cancel at the last moment. They "forget" their password or the commands for system use. They constantly report the system as malfunctioning.

These are not malevolent people. They are usually found to be those who have not had any input into the implementation, yet who are expected to use the new system and to support its use throughout the organization. They lack a basic understanding of how the system works, why they were included in the project, and have little motivation (other than fear of being seen as resistant) for learning the new behaviors required.

When asked about the problems regarding their behavior, people have said things like: "If this machine is so smart, it will catch these errors", "I'll show them that they still need me", "If we all have trouble with it, maybe they'll bring back the old way of doing things" and "I'll be darned if some machine will force me to change."

What is the common theme? It is simply one of frustration. When you don't understand how something works, when you don't know why you should change, when the change seems to increase rather than decrease your workload, and when you have nowhere to go to get help without getting punished (overtly or covertly), naturally you feel frustrated and angry. Who has not kicked a wastebasket or ripped up papers in frustration?

Who has not delayed a decision or feigned ignorance on occasion? Yet are we all irresponsible people?

In fact, if you take a broader look at the lives of most of your employees, you will see that they are fully responsible, decisionmaking adults. Many are responsible parents. Many are on boards of directors of voluntary organizations (often managing large budgets). Many contribute their efforts and knowledge to further any number of not-for-profit causes. So why do so many seem to need so much direction at work?

A major culprit, as noted earlier, is the organization itself. Most bureaucratically-based companies foster a dependent attitude in their employees. There are manuals and procedures for everything and exceptions are expected to be referred upward. Independent thought is not expected — moreover, often it is punished. People's areas of responsibility are so narrowly defined that they are unable to display their many competencies.

It is not easy to take the first step needed to allow employees to show what they can do. But only the manager can take this initiative. The employee who tries it on his or her own is the one who is referred to as "maverick" or "upstart".

There are many managers who encourage others to act independently and are promptly disappointed. Their first experience with participative decisionmaking, for example, turns into a complete fiasco. The issue is that when you allow others responsibility, you must also provide them with the tools and skills to function well.

For example, a manager who was new to a department wanted to help one of his employees upgrade her job classification. He truly believed that she was not being paid enough for the amount of responsibility her job entailed. So he asked her to rewrite her job description and submit it for reclassification and promised he would support her in any inquiries that came back. Imagine his dismay when she reacted in anger, frustration and expressed feelings of having been let down!

He thought he was treating her as a responsible adult. From her point of view, however, she was being set up. Here was a new manager, professing new management, but making her write the job description alone. She did not know on what criteria the jobs were rated. She had never written one in her life. Yet, if the re-rating were denied, she would have nowhere to turn. The classic double-bind. If she writes it and fails, it's her fault. If she doesn't write it, then she is demonstrating that she shouldn't be reclassified.

Luckily, it was possible to resolve the situation. The manager, when made aware of the impact and the double-bind that had been created, used the opportunity to talk about the issue (thus creating trust) and to teach how job descriptions are written. Working with the employee, he helped her create an outline. She wrote a first draft, which they reviewed together. Then, feeling that she had the information she needed to go forward, she petitioned for the re-rating and was successful.

Given the massive disruption that can be encountered during the introduction of the integrated office, there are many chances for awkward moments such as this. Too often, managers give opportunity (such as input in decisionmaking, job design, etc.) and yet deny the chance to learn how to do these things properly. Usually, time is the villain, as reflected in comments such as: "We don't have time to teach you about the impact of technology, but tell us what you need to do your job better." "We are too busy to allow you time for adequate training, but I want you to fully utilize what we have spent so much on." The examples are endless.

How, under these circumstances, can managers be convinced that their employees are independent and self-regulating? Examine your own career or look for instances where you, or someone you know, was in the non-managerial situation. Many female managers were once support staff; many male managers performed some sort of clerical or production job before entering management. Or you may have children doing that now. Were you, or are they, any less responsible or competent because of the title held? Or was it the situation and the lack of trust exhibited by your manager that made you seem so? In thinking about this, you may discover a willingness to take more of a risk with your employees.

Some Management Skills Can't Be Automated

These, then, cover the more general demands on management for the future. Managers and their organizations must encourage innovation, support participative decisionmaking and create the climate in which collaboration and collegiality flourish. To do so, they must accept employees as responsible, self-regulating adults. Let's now turn to some specific requirements for managing people in the context of the integrated office.

With the trend to more information processing and less production of tangible items, separating quality control from the work itself becomes difficult. Unless you are going to watch every keystroke, how will you know the quality of the data or information being input? Unless you monitor every operation, how will you know that the proper analytic tools are being applied to the data? Unless you receive paper copy, how will you know just what has been sent over the electronic mail system for which you were not an addressee? The issues are numerous.

This is not only a problem with information processing. The same can be said of service. We have noted the increased size of the service sector in the post-industrial age. But service is notoriously difficult to monitor for quality. Whether one receives value for money is a subjective judgement. As such, it is difficult to establish whether a particular service is being rendered well or not.

The inability of management to closely monitor quality will be an issue mainly for managers who attempt to continue using outmoded styles of management. If you have learned to be comfortable with the collaborative approach that has been discussed here, you will also find that the people who work for you, being responsible adults who are constantly concerned about the quality of their work, are using all the cues available to them to maintain high quality. Thus your main job will be to assist them when they feel they have insufficient information to perform their jobs, including the quality control aspect.

The introduction of the integrated office will create the situation where other systems, such as the performance appraisal system, will need to be reviewed and possibly revised. The manager's role in performance appraisal may change and each employee will need to be much more aware of how performance is judged and each person (manager, co-worker, and self) plays a role in increasing the quality of work performed. This will be looked at in more detail in a later chapter.

Another aspect of the more traditional management job will also change. Many managers spend a great deal of time collecting data or information from their employees and interpreting that data for transmission further up the line. This "gatekeeper" function is currently necessary to protect senior management from being swamped by the excess of information generated within the organization. It is now possible to create computer systems (so-called "expert systems") which emulate this analysis function.

The implication for managers is that senior management will not have to rely on a middle layer to perform analyses for them. Supported by the expert systems, they will be able to do analyses on whatever data they wish at whatever time they wish. The gatekeeper role will diminish in importance.

It may seem that there will be no role left for the middle manager. The truth is,

there will be less need for the traditional tasks of middle management — not for the people themselves.

There are many tasks not adequately handled now because everyone is too busy to do them. These mainly fall in the category of "people management". Less time will be spent policing quality and performance or opening and closing the gates for information. More will be spent in facilitating and ensuring that the "outside world" does not interfere with the employees' ability to get their jobs done.

The successful manager will assist people in getting the information and tools they need to do the job and will see that they have sufficient freedom to do all that they need to do. Providing the opportunity for people to be creative, innovative and collegial are examples of the new tasks. These managerial tasks are much more difficult than the traditional tasks. Working with data is more objective and often less threatening than dealing with "people issues". Managing the human issues is also the part of the job which can not be automated — therefore, the manager who wants to manage for a long term will invest the time and energy in learning how to do these new things well.

The introduction of the integrated office provides a marvelous opportunity for beginning the move to the new management style. In a time of change, it seems natural that new ways of working will be tried; so, there is less cynicism or suspicion about new behaviors. People are exhilarated by the opportunities created for trying new ways of working with new tools. Once experienced, most people will resist returning to former ways of working. It is not an easy style to introduce, but is most definitely worth the effort required.

Computer Aided or Computer Degraded? The Importance of Job Design

As managers, we are all concerned with organizational effectiveness. We have to be — our jobs depend on it. Effectiveness in organizations is a function of the right people doing the right things in the right way. The key to attracting and retaining the right people often lies in creating an environment that guides them towards doing the right things and in ensuring that they have the proper tools. Good job design is fundamental to achieving organizational effectiveness.

The way in which work is set up has been found to have a profound impact on the energy which a person will display for doing the job. In other words, job design can affect motivation and there is little doubt that motivation is a crucial factor in productivity. Since integrated office systems are often used to enhance productivity, the relationship between the integrated office and job design deserves close attention.

The devastating effect that poor job design can have on employee productivity was clearly shown by the study of the government office in Chapter Six. You may recall that during the introduction of new technology, management encouraged users to help design their office space, choose the equipment that would be used and provide input on various other matters. So what was the root of the problem? Let me explain here that the internal consulting group had requested the help of the personnel department in job design and, for various reasons, the assistance was denied. So they decided to visit other companies using the same equipment to learn how jobs were designed there. The result was the use, without modification, of job structures and task allocation used by a large marketing firm.

Within six months there had been considerable turnover in one section of the office, morale was down and productivity gains expected had failed to materialize. Through interviews and questionnaires, we looked at how motivating the various new jobs were. This analysis indicated that two out of three support staff sections now had jobs that were lower in the factors that are important to motivation than they had had before.

When these findings were reported, it was painfully obvious that something had gone wrong. Quickly, resources were allocated to discover the source of the problem and its solution. What was learned was that the jobs, as designed, were a good fit for a marketing environment but were totally unsuited for a government one. In the marketing organization, the people moved rapidly through the support function. Few were on the same job for more than a year due to transfers and promotions. Most employees were well educated, highly ambitious and mobile. By contrast, in the government office, stability was the norm. People stayed with the same section for years and rarely received (or expected) promotions. They were not particularly ambitious, although they were productive and desired to do good work.

Under these conditions, it is not surprising that the jobs that were satisfying and motivating in one setting were not found to be so in the other. The nub of the matter is that management thought that job design was a factor of the technology, rather than of the tasks to be done and the people who would be doing them.

Proper job design begins with an understanding of the organization and the direction in which it is moving. Only then can the tasks that need to be accomplished to attain the objectives be derived. These tasks are then analyzed — ideally, by those currently doing the tasks — to determine the appropriate way to combine them into meaningful jobs and groups of jobs. People who are currently employed can then be evaluated to see which of the jobs can be done by them. Only then should the analysis of the tools needed to do the jobs be undertaken.

To begin with the tools available and then design jobs that make use of these tools is illogical and self-defeating.

However, it is not quite that simple. This progression from organization to job to tool is actually one cycle of a repeated process. Over time, two major forces contribute to the need for further changes. First, the environment is constantly placing new demands on the organization. The market moves. Competitors revise their products. The economy swings. All of these call for constant reevaluation of the organization's mission and objectives. Second, the experience within the organization and the lessons taught by this experience create opportunities for doing "new things in new ways". This is one of the most powerful dynamics of the integrated office.

For example, one health insurance organization found it had a wealth of information that could be packaged for the use of researchers and health care providers. Before there was computer access to the files, this information was too costly to analyze. By using the new technology, the people in the enterprise have been able to refocus their efforts. In the past, their jobs were geared to paying insurance claims; now, in addition to claims payment, they work with health officials, hospitals and researchers to seek areas of unusually high cost or high health risk. Together these workers attempt to actively manage costs and threats before they get out of hand. The introduction of technology presented an opportunity to reevaluate the approach to jobs and tasks and to change some jobs from being administratively oriented to action oriented.

An organization which encourages innovation and provides the tools to support it is usually a font of new ideas, methods and approaches. These in turn must be reintegrated into the planning process so that in future planning cycles, the organization finds itself able to include objectives which it could not contemplate before.

Examples of new technology's ability to change the organization's way of working or its focus can be found in many facets of the integrated office. Text management through sophisticated word processing systems has been found to greatly enhance the creativity of people working with the systems. Many authors, have found this to be the case. In some schools of journalism, creative-writing students are *required* to work with computer-based text processing systems because the professors have found that the quality of submissions from the students is greatly improved. New financial modeling tools help people in analyzing opportunities and problems confronting the company. The new communication capabilities encourage the collaboration of people who have never been able to work together because of time and distance constraints. They may create proposals for new work or develop new products that would not have been contemplated.

When an organization develops new skills, it can use them to increase its competitive advantage. In the process, of course, the objectives will again change and this will set off a new round of examining the tasks to be done and how best to organize jobs to accomplish them. So we can see that with the introduction of integrated office systems, job design becomes, indeed, never ending.

What Is Meant by 'Good' Job Design

Many failures in introducing new technology have been traced to the failure to properly redesign the jobs affected by the use of new tools. So we can benefit from understanding the findings of job design researchers. Research in the field of job design has focused on what constitutes "good" jobs, that is, jobs that are productive and motivating. As noted earlier, these two characteristics go together, but we do not know whether being productive makes one feel motivated or vice versa. The relationship between the two factors is, indeed, more complex. Since we do not know the direction of the influence, we must concentrate our efforts on creating jobs that include both components.

Job design can be looked at from two perspectives. First is the relationship between an individual and his or her particular job. Second is the wider social context and the factors that influence job design with respect to constellations of jobs and groups of people who perform the jobs. We will look at each.

What are the things which determine whether an individual job is motivating and productive? Richard Hackman and his associates at Yale University have explored this issue for several years and have derived a set of factors which can be used to assess the design of individual jobs. There are five items of primary importance: skill variety, task identity, task significance, autonomy and the amount of performance feedback provided by the job itself. We will explore each in turn.

Skill variety refers to the number and difficulty of skills and the variety of talents required to perform a job. There can be quite a range in this variable. A keypunch operator may use very few skills and those used are likely of very low level (mostly motor). An executive, on the other hand, uses many different skills (reading, writing, presenting, analyzing, consulting, leading, etc.) and most of them are at a high intellectual level. Most office workers have jobs which fall somewhere in between.

The introduction of integrated office systems can be used as an opportunity to increase the skill variety of the job. However, in some of the less successful implementations, the number of skills required were *decreased*. For example, when word processing equipment was first introduced, it was very expensive, especially when compared to the typewriters being replaced. Consequently, many organizations, seeking to get maximum use of this new equipment, designed jobs so that machine use was very high — eight hours a day, or more if there was a second shift. Typists were retrained to do "power typing", very fast entry of text with little regard for accuracy. Proofreading and correction were performed by other people. These typists experienced a great reduction in skill variety and, in fact, considered themselves to have been "de-skilled", a term which refers to the lessening of opportunities to use skills on the job. As one person whose department underwent such a change told me, "That equipment should enhance our lives. But all we have is typing pool — doing the same thing all day long!"

There are many examples where the introduction of new technology has had a more positive impact. For instance, in the last chapter we looked at a firm that successfully introduced computerized drafting equipment for its engineers and drafting staff. In this case, the drafting staff were trained to modify plans and to make minor engineering decisions within pre-established guidelines. For them, this represented an increase in the skills required to do the job.

Finally, the knowledge acquired in learning to use integrated office systems in an effective manner is a valuable new skill in itself.

If not altered by a simultaneous reduction in other skill demands, a systems introduction should result in increased skill variety. For most people then, the introduction of new office equipment can lead to an enhancement of their job.

The second variable, task identity, refers to the degree to which a job has a "wholeness" or "completeness". Can the person doing the job recognize a complete piece of work or is the person working on a single part which doesn't make sense by itself? To a large degree, office jobs have traditionally been fairly complete. While it is true that some clerical jobs were broken up into smaller and smaller pieces — such as a bank employee keypunching check amounts — many more were a integral part of the whole organizational task. Certainly this has been the case for secretaries, most analysts, managers and professionals.

Everyone with responsibility for the introduction of integrated office systems must be sure that the urge to break jobs into smaller pieces, in order to have people concentrate on only one aspect of a job, is resisted. This can happen when people who are "generalists" such as secretaries are turned into "specialists" such as word processing operators. In the government case example in Chapter Six, the word processing operators initially were not permitted to speak with those doing the writing, and when work had to be revised, it did not necessarily go back to the person who had done it originally. Thus, these people did not see any task through from beginning to end and could not feel any significant amounts of task identity.

Task significance, the third factor involved in good job design, is related to and yet is somewhat different from task identity. This variable deals with the extent to which the job is perceived to have a substantial impact on the lives or work of other people and on the attainment of the company's objectives.

When jobs are restructured and broken up to maximize equipment use, it is not uncommon to find that some of the new jobs have a low task significance. The employee no longer follows a piece of work through from beginning to end and consequently loses sight of the importance of his or her particular contribution to the process. Just as an assembly line worker after the one-millionth bolt tightening may no longer care just how important that bolt is to the assembly of the whole car, so too may the terminal operator become cynical about how her or his input affects the end product.

For example, one data center hired a very bright college student for a summer. She was assigned the task of typing figures into the accounts payable system, which then automatically initiated the processing and printing of checks. She received approved payment vouchers containing all the necessary information. She performed her data entry task well all summer but on the last day instructed the computer to issue a check for seven million dollars payable to Donald Duck and authorized by Goofy! The check went through and was finally caught at the bank. This woman had lost sight of her contribution to the process and the impact of her actions. Her departing act of sabotage was meant as a protest against the job. She never dreamed that she had the power to make anything happen. She assumed that her acts were unimportant and trivial. She did not realize that her "humor" would cause the organization considerable wasted time and money to reconstruct records. Nor did she anticipate the embarrassment to the company when the act became public.

Of course, the impact was not as serious as if the entering of false data had taken place in a hospital. In a hospital setting, the records form the basis for, among other things, treatment decisions. Hospitals have built checks into their information systems to identify the malicious entry of data, but there is no system that is foolproof. Every organization is ultimately dependent on the goodwill of its employees. Years of accumulated goodwill can be jeopardized when the people doing jobs are not motivated because of the lack of task significance.

Any failure in this area becomes even more significant when we consider the impact on integrated office systems. The fact that they are integrated means that the information is shared; therefore, the importance of accuracy is heightened. But if people do not realize where they, as individuals, fit and how their job is related to the whole, then they will be less able to assess the impact of what they do and may have little reason to care about the quality of their work. Information entered at one point is used for organizational decisionmaking throughout the company; therefore, its accuracy and timeliness is very important.

However, it is very difficult to demonstrate this to people who see their task as "copying these numbers onto a computer screen".

The fourth factor that contributes to good job design is the degree of autonomy experienced. People feel that it is important for them to have a degree of control over such aspects of the job as scheduling the pace of their work, deciding how to perform the work and how to resolve the problems that inevitably arise in any job. This feeling of independence, or power to control, is what we mean by autonomy.

With all that we have said about the "new" employees, it is logical that autonomy should rank high on their list of desired criteria for good jobs. Better educated and brought up on Spock — both the doctor of child care fame and the Star Trek character — these people expect to have some control over what they do and how they do it. Interestingly, this variable is one of the most difficult to rate objectively. If a person has a feeling of job independence, then the rating will be high. If the employee feels that he or she has little control over the job, then the rating will be low, regardless of how another "objective" person might rate it.

Integrated office systems can either contribute to autonomy or diminish it, depending on how the systems are designed and used. If programmed to measure many minute details, then they will seem to take freedom away, regardless of what the data is used for. For example, it is possible to measure the number of keystrokes per minute made by an operator. This, on occasion, has been used for systems evaluation in some word processing projects. When this data is being collected, the operators feel their privacy is being invaded. Even if the data are not used for performance appraisal, the operators hesitate to vary their rate of typing over the day for fear that the times when they are going at peak speed will be used as baselines for everyday performance. Though it is human nature to perform more efficiently at certain times of the day, there is, nonetheless, a reluctance to have a machine measure this.

One telephone operator explains the difference between working on a "cord board" and the new computerized equipment which was used by long distance operators:

> On a cord board, what you had was a situation of operators sitting side by side. And you, in fact, had complete control over the timing of the calls, you had complete control over the amount of time spent on the call, and you did have also control of the calls that you chose to answer, of course, because they were designated on the cord board with strips — coin boxes, hotels. So you had a basic control over the way you worked, the pace that you worked at. What's happened with (this new system) is that you have no control over the situation. The calls are flying at you, and I've been sitting there in some

instances where I don't even have time to take a deep breath between calls. And when you have calls popping in and out, in and out, you just handle them as quickly as you can and just hope to get rid of them and maybe get a five second rest between that and the next one coming up. You can't cough, because you could very well cough in someone's ear, which is not at all pleasant. At this point, you would want to possibly pull out of your position. Well, this then indicates at the In Charge (the supervisor's location) that one position is in the 'made busy' mode, and they will promptly depress a key that will tell them what position is in the 'made busy' mode, and will look for it, and ask you why you're in made busy. In which case you would explain that you either have to sneeze or burp or whatever. To sum it up, the difference with the cord board and (the new system) is so great that I can't even find a parallel in any way, and it's been crushing for a lot of people."[5]

It is possible to collect performance data if it is essential. To do so, some or all of the employees should be members of a participative design and evaluation team. During the design process, they will gain an understanding that the information is necessary for the organization to evaluate its expenditure, to learn from the implementation process and to use as a basis for the intelligent redesign of jobs. When the employees accept the validity of the purpose to which the information will be put, they are more likely to cooperate with the data collection process. The team should also design the processes by which the information will be collected and used. As well, they need to design safeguards so that the data will not be available to set performance standards unless agreed upon by the employees themselves. Using this approach, organizations have found that performance information collected is often far more accurate than what would have been collected without the support of the employees. This procedure is also a good example of how to use the participative approach for designing new jobs.

Integrated office systems have the potential to reduce the autonomy not only of the clerical staff, but also of the middle managers and staff analysts. When senior managers find they have direct access to information through the new systems, some of them may begin to do their own analyses, thus challenging or "Monday morning quarterbacking" their staff. The staff may begin to feel that, not only do they have to do their analyses, they now have to guess how the manager might do it and perform the analysis in that manner as well in order to "cover all bases". This may not be all bad. It encourages staff to understand how their managers think and to present information in a manner which is consistent with those thought processes. It does, however, become a problem when the staff feels less freedom and a challenge to their professionalism

— which, it turns out, is usually unintended by senior management.

The fifth variable is how much performance feedback does the job itself provide. It is impossible to improve performance without some idea of how well one is currently performing.

The greater the amount of information concerning performance that can be gathered by just doing the job, the better the job design.

No one likes to be told by someone else that their work is less than superior. But everyone wants to know how she or he is doing and often there is no way to find out other than feedback systems, ideally designed into the job itself.

For example, typists who proofread their own work see errors and poor layout immediately, without the intervention of another party. Returned letters, covered with red circles, provide the same information, but in a form which is less likely to encourage improvement. Coming from someone else, it causes the typist to feel embarrassed and angry. And a person who is angry is much less able to learn how to avoid making the same mistakes.

Integrated office systems can provide a tremendous opportunity for more direct feedback to employees. That is, when the appropriate software is used, the new technology can increase the feedback from the job itself. Implicit in the idea of feedback is the understanding that the information is for the use of the employee to monitor and improve performance. If the data on performance is used by other people for appraisal, then there is less chance that it will be a motivating factor, because its use reduces the autonomy of the individual. So merely collecting data regarding quality or quantity won't in itself create a more motivating job. The employee must also exercise control over the use of that information.

Individual performance data, available on a minute-to-minute basis, is considered by most to be a private matter. Such information is not currently available in most organizations, so the question becomes why *should* others have it just because the technology makes it possible? A mistake often made in implementing new systems is to make use of every "bell and whistle" available, no matter whether it is relevant to increased organizational effectiveness. More humane implementations now encourage employees to disable any program — for example, the collection and reporting of performance data — that they feel is a threat to privacy, if they have not agreed in advance to the use of that program. In this, as in many technology situations, "Can does not imply ought"; that is, just because you can collect the data does not mean that you ought to!

These are five factors you can use to judge whether any job is likely to be both motivating and productive. Of course, the relationship between the individual and the job is not the only thing you need to consider. The broader social context within which the job is located must also be looked at to determine the relationships between jobs and how the people assigned to the tasks will interact with one another. Changes in jobs alter these relationships and can have a profound impact on the ability of individuals to perform effectively.

Social Effects are Important

People work to meet a variety of needs, some of which are unrelated to job performance. But we all know that when we feel frustrated and our needs are not being met, we are less likely to perform well. So it is important to understand how employees' need satisfaction will be affected when you change established job relationships. For example, when an electronic messaging system is introduced, executives send messages directly to each other, bypassing the secretaries who previously set up the phone contacts. Those secretaries who have a high need for social contact may feel that their jobs have been impoverished. Not only have they lost an important source of information about what their bosses are working on, but they have also lost the opportunity to informally compare notes with the other secretaries about what is happening in the company. It may sound petty, but systems implementations have failed for reasons such as eliminating joint coffee breaks. Ignoring the social context of work is very dangerous.

Some elements of the integrated office systems will increase social contacts and decrease others. Through electronic messaging it is possible to have contact with people who were previously unavailable because of time and geographic differences. On the other hand, at times this same technology makes face-to-face meetings or telephone calls less necessary. It is important to understand where the changes will take place, to anticipate the loss of some contacts and to ensure that there are enough other benefits available to users that the loss, while regretted, is also understood and accepted. Users of integrated office systems have found that the meetings that *are* held are more productive and satisfying because everyone is able to be prepared and relevant information is easily shared both before and during the meeting. However, those individuals for whom social contact is a key factor in satisfaction on the job will need to be encouraged to find other ways to meet these needs and those of the organization at the same time.

Getting information on this social need is not always easy. But you must learn to appreciate the need for and the value to the organization of such behaviors as unscheduled interaction. People will create new communication forms, such as computer grapevines, that will help them get the information they need. If misunderstood, they may be punished for using the system in "unauthorized" ways when, in fact, the use was beneficial to the enterprise.

For example, one stockbrokerage company, on merging with another and bringing new systems to the smaller one, found that the computer mail system was being used to discuss, among other things, the weather at the various offices around the country. Word came down from "on high" that this system was to be used for business messaging only. What was not understood, however, was that most of the people on the system did not know the people in New York office who were their new bosses and were using this social commentary (or gossip sometimes) to develop a working relationship with them. It was, in fact, no different from the typical conversation opening of "How are you?" or "Is it cold enough for you?" But, of course, here it was being done in print rather than verbally.

The results were not what the company expected. Without this friendly interchange, people at the branches felt distant and alone. They felt that the people in the New York office were too important to be bothered with "my little problem". Only important information was to be communicated; yet the branch personnel were not sufficiently trained to be able to determine the relative importance of various symptoms. So, some organizationally important information was not communicated and, increased equipment failures were the result — a rather large problem for brokers trying to enter customers' orders. In addition, the people operating the order system felt more alienated and frustrated than before.

One major change in the design of jobs that is possible with the support of electronic equipment is the development of jobs designed around groups rather than individuals. This is a positive change that supports the new environment of collaboration and cooperation. Also, task teams and groups with many skills can be more flexible and responsive, again behaviors which are needed within the new organization. And, of course, for jobs which had previously been done in isolation, these team-based jobs add a social component that is both organizationally important and usually welcomed by the individual.

There has been considerable experimentation with work groups as a basis for work restructuring. It has been found that, when properly designed and implemented, this approach results in large gains for the workers and the organization.

The work group approach is based on the concept of "redundancy of functions". That is to say, each person is trained to perform many tasks and so can help out other members of the team when her or his own workload permits. In contrast, the traditional approach is called "redundancy of parts" which means that each person is trained for only one task. When one person is overloaded with work, other workers are not easily switched over to help. Alternatively, when there is too little work, the single skill person is underutilized.

For example, in many offices the work of the support staff is based on the traditional approach. There are file clerks, receptionists, secretaries, mail clerks and so on. Rarely are these people cross-trained. If there is a lot of typing to be done, the organization must hire temporary typists, even though there may be others workers in the same office who are not busy. There are clearly losses involved with this method of work organization. But it is justified because of the different pay rates for the various positions — mail clerks are "cheaper" than secretaries.

The group approach requires a different perspective on work and working. It assumes that everyone wants to be productive and to feel effectively utilized, and that this is valued by the organization. Also, it assumes that people want to improve their skills and to learn new things and that this, too, is valued. But it also recognizes that people expect to be rewarded for their skills and experience.

Work groups are set up around a particular set of tasks. The skills needed to perform all the tasks are assessed and the group, as a whole, must ensure that it can do all the tasks. Usually, the group members have a variety of skills and over time these will be taught to one another. Then, as work comes to the group, members can be assigned tasks according to the needs at that moment. People can switch tasks in response to changing work demands on the group and the group members experience a more regular level of workload demand. The situation of some people being underutilized and of others being overworked within the same group is less likely to happen.

For example, let's take another look at the government support group case discussed in Chapter Six to see how these principles might be applied. The support staff would be designated as a work group responsible for the administrative work of that office. They would map out the tasks to be done and the skills needed to do them. Group members would identify the skills that they did not possess but wished to learn, and they would then develop a plan for acquiring these skills. Pay would be based on the number of skills possessed and whether they were used in a particular day. Rarely would all the members of a group acquire all the skills needed to be in the top pay grade. The natural combination of turnover, promotions and the decision of some members not to take on that challenge have been found to provide a built-in stabilizing effect on the average wage scale. Assignment to jobs would be a responsibility of the group. Work assignments could be changed daily or continued over time, as determined by the group. But assignments would be changed as workloads in certain jobs varied.

In essence, this is the "professional" approach to work. Professionals such as doctors, lawyers, dentists and accountants base their hourly or project rates on the skills and experience they possess. As a client, you may never use some of their skills, but you pay for them just the same.

There is no reason that this same approach cannot be applied to other kinds of work. In the case discussed in the last chapter, where computer-aided drafting was introduced in the engineering and drafting division of a manufacturing company, the draftspeople were formed into a work team. They established the tasks needed to be done to gain mastery of the system and to fully realize the benefits available. These tasks were graded in steps and with the mastery of each step the individual draftsperson received an increment in pay. Each person attained a minimum level of skill, which included such tasks as learning to use the system for normal drafting and using the system to make minor changes to plans. At higher levels, a group member might learn to write new programs for innovative uses of the computer and to maintain the equipment.

Thus the group, over time, became quite self-sufficient, reducing the need for the organization to contract for help. Not every skill was used every day and not every draftsperson chose to complete every step. So there remained differentials within the group, but these were by choice and thus created no problem or resentment. In addition to reducing the need for other specialists, the organization found that the group could handle a wide variety of jobs. The cross-learning meant members could process work more accurately and quickly and so response time and error rate were both reduced.

This approach works best when you have a group of people with similar educational and experience backgrounds working on relatively similar tasks. It is ideal for such parts of the organization as administrative support and specialized pools like drafting or programming staffs. It is more of a challenge to apply when the skills to be shared are not easily taught on the job. For example, a group of lawyers which included tax, real estate and corporate specialists, would be unlikely to begin teaching each other their areas of expertise and, in fact, such a move might not bring the organization any meaningful gains. But the case where engineers and draftsmen worked as a team on projects has been very success-ful once initial scepticism was overcome.

As we saw at the beginning of this chapter, the introduction and proliferation of integrated office systems has an *ongoing* impact on the jobs within organizations. The ability to do new things in new ways allows the organization to introduce new products and services and to organize in innovative ways. These changes then again alter the way jobs and tasks are done and the tools needed to perform them. The constant evolution of technology introduces opportunities for upgrading tools which in turn can cause further alterations in the way things are done.

Therefore, there is an *ongoing* need to monitor how jobs are being performed and to keep their design consistent with the task needs. As jobs are redesigned, there are many opportunities to give employees new skills and to restructure work groups in more productive and indepen-dent ways. Retraining of these employees is, of course, a constant challenge.

The benefits for the organization are many. Building on the increased flexibility created by the use of new tools and the skill-building of employees, the company can continually increase its ability to meet the new market demands and to reap the rewards that the marketplace offers to those who are the most responsive.

The Importance of Space and Furniture Design

The introduction of integrated office systems invariably results in some changes to the physical design of the office. The new tools are shaped differently than those of the past and the old furniture will not do. The needs for different wiring and lighting also create change. As well, the analysis that indicates the need for the new tools often reveals the need to improve the effectiveness of the layout of offices and departments. Too often, this aspect of redesign is separated from the job design and systems design. Consequently, the organization loses the opportunity to integrate and reinforce the other changes taking place.

If the introduction of new technology is also seen as an opportunity to encourage other changes in management style and employee behavior, then the impact of physical design cannot be overlooked. Proper physical design can encourage communication, movement and create the feeling of increased freedom and decreased surveillance. There are ways to use space so there is a reduction in the distance felt between people in the various levels of the organization. This can be used to support collegiality and collaborative efforts. And there are designs that increase the diversity of activities which can be easily performed, thus supporting the innovative use of tools to accomplish a variety of tasks.

As with job design, then, the design of space should be closely tied to the analysis of the objectives of the organization. Space design will be one of the strategies to be used to accomplish these objectives. The participation of those who will be most involved in using the space is necessary to ensure that the strategies and tactics are translated into designs that are appropriate for to those people who must work in these environments.

We now realize that the design of interior space has a great impact on the behavior of people. In many companies, office design is the responsibility of people trained only in the physical aspects of design, who then make decisions about the allocation of space based solely on cost and status considerations and with little knowledge of its impact on the occupants. In the past, facilities management people developed guidelines for office space design that focused on the status level of the person who would inhabit that space — so many dollars per square foot or so many square feet per organizational level.

In the future, the "space planners" hired by an organization will have a larger perspective than just short-term cost and status; indeed, it is likely that teams of consultants, including space planners, architectural designers and human factors professionals will respond to requests for office planning assistance. They will be required to help the organizational decisionmakers understand the effects of decisions regarding lighting, acoustics, space, thermal comfort, wiring and related aspects of interior design. Managers will want to include them on planning teams along with representatives of other disciplines to ensure that decisions reinforce and support each other.

Sending Messages via Design

Proper design can increase desired behaviors and help eliminate others. The design of space and its furnishing communicates to people how the decisionmakers in the organization feel, think and function. That is, it conveys messages concerning culture, roles and norms. Thus, if you wish to move your organization toward more flexibility and innovation, there are physical design decisions that can help or hinder this transition.

The arrangement of personal space in an office often reflects the philosophy of the person or persons most responsible for that arrangement. To demonstrate this for yourself, look at various office furniture arrangements for managers who have discretion regarding this factor. See who has the desk so that it is a barrier to anyone who enters and who has the desk placed at an angle so that visitors can approach the person directly. There is usually a relationship between how the desk is set and how approachable the person is or wants to be, though interpretation of this relationship is not as straightforward as some believe. That is, while it is true that a person who is not an approachable manager may "erect a barrier" in the form of placing the desk between him or herself and any visitor, some very approachable people may do the same thing in order to help them create distance and thus increase their ability to manage the amount of intrusion they allow others. The managers who have a genuine "open door" policy and are believed by their employees to be easy to talk to will often have desks that are not barriers and have a chair by the side of the desk for those who want to talk personally. Conversely, those who have read books on the topic and wish to manipulate the impression they give others will deliberately position the furniture to create an impression that is not necessarily reflective of how they feel about their space.

Work groups exhibit the same characteristics. When a group is very interactive and supportive, they will usually arrange their furniture in a very open pattern that is easy to move around. If they see themselves as an unusual group within the culture of the organization, such as a pilot or experimental group, they will often erect barriers between themselves and the outside. For example, in one case, the pilot group moved all of the office partitions to the outside of the group boundaries. Though that meant they had to give up individual offices, they saw it as an opportunity to increase intimacy as the group learned to work together in new ways and, at the same time, to "protect" them from intrusion by the rest of the organization.

Employees watch very carefully to see what management truly believes, as opposed to what they say they believe. One of the places that they test management's statements is with respect to decisions made about space design.

For example, the senior management of one company decided it would support only those applications of new technology which enhanced the working environment of its employees. The secretary to one vice-president got word processing equipment that overwhelmed her office and so a space redesign was required. A design firm from another city was called in, many weeks were spent in design and a total reconstruction of her office was done at great expense. The new office was beautiful and looking down "executive row" was a delight.

Only one problem. The office was horrible to work in. Smoked glass walls had been added to isolate her from the other secretaries. Lighting had been reduced to a point where she could not see her phone to dial it. Her walls were now all hard surface that reflected noise and thus magnified the sound of the printer and directed it straight across the hall into her boss's office. To adapt, she had to add multiple mufflers (printer cover and pad) to control the noise and a clamp-on light. Other expenses were incurred to help recover from this "improvement".

Neither the secretary nor her boss were ever consulted during the redesign. Participation was not even thought of, as the space planners were to "work their magic". And what messages were sent to the organization? That what we say (that we care about our employees and their work environment) is somewhat less than what we mean (our main concern is that things *look* right). That people will not have input into decisions that affect their work and working environment. That the criteria we use to judge the competence of consultants is "how it looks, not what it does".

Of course, these are not the messages management *meant* to send. But they had divorced space planning from other aspects of dealing with new technology and thus just didn't think of the impact of what they did. But the employees were very aware that the response to this one person's problem was an indication of how their own problems would be dealt with when the time came. And the indication they got was what management had promised. A new communication problem was born. This example illustrates the difficulty in living up to stated values and the necessity of always testing decisions for how they will be interpreted.

The Basics

As implied in the last example, there are some special design considerations for a large-scale introduction of microprocessor-based technology such as integrated office systems. While these systems are much less sensitive than the mainframe data processing computers, they still have special requirements and create some problems for the office worker.

In a typical design, each person has a workstation consisting of a keyboard and screen the size of a small television. Additionally, some people will have a printer, which may be the size of an electric typewriter or larger. A few systems also include a built-in telephone, but most people will still have a regular telephone on their desks for the near future.

Thus, the first problem presented is what to do with all this new equipment. It covers a third to a half of most desks and the whole desk if a printer is included. If an electric typewriter is being removed, you might think that there would be little need to change from a size perspective. But this is not the case. Experience has shown that you can expect a 5 to 20 percent increase in work surface area needed, because the typical typewriter area is about two-thirds of the depth that is needed to accommodate the typical computer terminal. As well, the dream that this equipment will replace paper and you won't need anything except the terminal has not and probably will never be realized. In fact, there may be an increased need for space to accomodate the extra paper generated by the high speed printers. So people must have room to continue working on tasks that do not require the terminal.

The management and professional staff may, in some organizations, present a particular problem. If they demand furniture compatible with their level in the organization, they will quickly find that the range of furniture available that is not strictly functional (based on the needs of the equipment) is limited indeed. Some implementations have run into trouble because managers have resisted th idea of desktop terminals, and yet the terminals are not easily used if placed on credenzas.

If there are to be a number of terminals in one space, there is also a problem with temperature and noise. Both the units and the people operating them generate heat, so temperature levels can rise quickly. The motors of the disc drives may sometimes be heard. Several units together will noticeably raise the temperature and noise level of a room. Printers present a particularly difficult noise problem.

When many people are acquiring new systems simultaneously, the problems of heat, noise, lighting and wire management are more acute. When word processing pools were first formed, these settings looked very much like a factories: noisy, hot places in which individual people, mindlessly performing repetitive tasks, are attached to machines. Obviously, this kind of situation will not promote the behaviors we want to encourage in the future. But if insufficient attention is paid to the problem, we will continue to see these unhappy environments.

A more subtle problem is created when the new systems disrupt the social interaction patterns of the office. When conversion is complete and a great deal of information is available on the system, there is less need to go to filing cabinets. When electronic messaging is actively used, there is less need to pop into the office down the hall to check something out. When calendars are accessible through the system, there are fewer phone calls to set up meetings.

Separately, these may seem trivial. Taken together, however, they mean that there is less interaction between people. On your way to the filing cabinet you often speak to some of the people you pass. In setting up meetings, secretaries are also creating working relationships. Each interaction creates the opportunity to pass information, often information needed to do the job better. The new technology may decrease social contact, with the result that some employees may find that their social needs are less well met. This has lead to a build up of resentment toward the system. Managers can ensure that adequate social contact is maintained by supporting the new spontaneous ways of meeting the social and informational needs that will emerge. For each organization and unit, different behaviors will be seen; your job will be to avoid punishing a new behavior just because you don't see its relevance to the given task. Remember our example of the stockbroker's office where the new behavior involved talking about the weather — elimination of these messages reduced the ability of people to feel comfortable inquiring about problems they were facing.

The need for social contact must be recognized and ways found to ensure that informal meetings can continue to occur. For all the jokes about socializing at the water fountains, copying machines and coffee stations, it is recognized that these are important aspects of organizational communication patterns. Of course, bulletin boards also provide an opportunity for people to communicate. Use the services of a space planning professional who understands these needs and demand that these needs be met if you want to design the most effective organization possible.

When there is less need to move around just to get the tasks done, the design of the space should encourage movement and interaction to ensure that informal communication links are maintained. Gathering spaces should be included in the plans and decisions such as centralizing copying (usually in the basement!) should be assessed for their impact on communication and interaction as well as on the basis of straight cost/benefit impact.

It is important that the new tools not be the sole consideration when you are looking at the impact of redesign on space. For example, it is true that VTDs are easier to read and less of a strain for the user if the light is not too bright behind or above them. So it is often recommended that overall lighting be reduced, sometimes by as much as 50 percent, and that the users be given individual lights which can be focused on the papers on the desk without disrupting the screen display.

Knowing this fact, one company took it to the extreme, installing a new word processing unit in an old supply closet in which the bulbs from the overhead lights had been removed. The woman who was trying to learn to use the machine sat in the closet, reading the training manual by the light of a small bedside-type lamp. Is it any wonder she felt that the new equipment was alienating and didn't want to use it very much? While few organizations would go to such extremes, the same principle also operates on a more subtle level and this is more difficult to avoid.

For example, there are certain recommended levels of illumination for various tasks. Working at a VDT requires less illumination than working at a drafting table, for instance. Few people realize, however, that when a certain level of illumination is specified for a new office space, it is a common engineering practice to provide considerably more illumination. The engineering perspective is that the illumination should be at the required level three years after installation. So the calculations for lighting requirements include the expected reduction in light caused by accumulation of dust and the aging of the bulbs. This means that for at least three years, workers in that area are subjected to lighting that is too bright for their needs.

There are ways to overcome these problems. For instance, some lighting systems can measure the illumination in any area, including sunlight and intensity of the bulbs, and will increase or decrease the amount of light provided to constantly maintain a desired level. In fact, these systems also save unnecessary energy cost and thus can be cost-competitive with other options. But if the people making lighting decisions do not understand the need for these considerations, they will most likely continue to install the systems with which they are already familiar.

For those who spend a great deal of time using the terminal, there are specific considerations regarding design. Just as there are special chairs and tables for typists and draftspeople, so too there are special kinds of furniture which make the terminal operator's job easier. Features to look for include adjustable worksurface heights, footstools and individually controlled light sources. One of the most important considerations is the chair selected. Proper support of legs and back, easy adjustability, stable, and appropriate to the task (swiveling and rolling) and all required. Choosing the proper chair can be the most cost-effective step taken.

In addition, some workstations are easier to work with for longer periods. Some features which may prove attractive are antiglare screens and keyboards, intensity controls, control over screen colors, audible key clicks, palm rests, fully tiltable screens, and movable (or "detached") keyboards.

The criteria used in making decisions about these and other aspects of physical design must reflect the aims set out very early in the implementation process. As was pointed out in the implementation chapters, a key job of the task force is to make clear what the introduction of new technology is expected to accomplish in terms of productivity, effectiveness and satisfaction. It must take the stance that people are individuals with individual work methods. There is no one best way to do a task; rather, each person should be equipped with tools that allow him or her to perform in the manner best suited personally. So decision criteria must emphasize flexiblity and adaptability.

The physical aspects of the way people work are not the only considerations necessary. While it may be true that working with VDT near windows causes people to strain their eyes more, for an individual who abhors working in a windowless room, the physical strain may be preferred to the psychological strain experienced when working away from windows. There are many such tradeoffs in design. The person who must work with the equipment should be encouraged to experiment and find the work setup that is the best individual compromise.

In many European countries, legislation sponsored by unions and other employee groups has been passed that defines the characteristics of workstations that may be considered "fit" for users. The standards set are, for the most part, not currently met by the majority of North American equipment and this should cause some concern here. While it is a fact that some of these standards are now being challenged by ergonomic specialists and legislation may be changed as a result, it remains true that those most vocal about creating standards (in this case, the unions) will usually be able to establish the standards most favorable to their own needs. Traditionally, standards for health and safety issues have been set in Europe and then imported into North America. Already, legislation has been introduced in the U.S. and Canada that is likely to be passed in some form in the near future.

Every change, even change for the better, carries with it some unknown effects that will prove to be less than ideal. This exploration of the possible impacts of the physical design of space and of the use of new technology is meant to heighten your awareness of what may happen. After all, to manage the impacts you must understand them. With each change, choices are made. Having adequate information, so that appropriate questions at least get asked, helps ensure that these choices are made knowingly and with acceptance of the tradeoffs involved. To survive, organizations must go forward. At issue is the speed, direction and timing of that movement. For success, the organization must move ahead as a unit. If technological change outpaces the social evolution or the physical ability to handle the change, the organization will not experience the gains promised by the technology.

Fitting the Parts Together: The Role of Organization Design

So far in this section we have been focusing on how to manage the organizational changes that are coming. Management style, job design and space design have been shown to be important components of managing the change process. One additional factor, organization design, needs to be addressed.

Consider the case of the organization that decided to move its corporate headquarters to a new location several hundred miles away. Senior management recognized that this presented a number of opportunities to institute other changes at the same time. The very centralized and traditional character of the enterprise was to be altered, to one less formal and more risk-taking. With this in mind, the new headquarters designed was significantly different from the one being left — it had fewer levels, was more of a "campus" setting and allowed for greater interaction among employees. To facilitate the "cultural change", mission and objective statements were altered to reflect the desired new behavior and these were well communicated to the employees. Several pilot projects were initiated to explore whether the new technology could enhance both the change in approach and productivity.

Two years after the move nothing had changed. Senior management was still seen as distant and insular; traditional approaches to management continued to frustrate any less conventional approaches to markets or to managing others. The perception of the company by the financial community remained unchanged and the new technology purchased was used in very traditional ways and did not meet the cost justifications put forth for its purchase. Productivity gains were realized only by cutting staff, a very traditional way to achieve short-term gains.

Analysis shows that the organization design remained unaltered. Although the building was designed to be informal, the old, formal rules for space allocation and furnishings were used. Although increased communication between levels was desired, the same reporting relationships and communication vehicles were retained. Although risk-taking was to be encouraged, the old reward and performance evaluation system remained in place. And although new technology could have been used to decentralize decisionmaking, tight central control was exercised in selecting software for the equipment. In general, no change was made to the organization design.

Organization design involves the development of the structure through which other management components will live. It is the framework which enhances or diminishes other efforts to improve productivity. This framework is not a static structure; rather, it is a constantly evolving set of relationships and influence bases which changes as the demands on the organization (and its responses to these demands) evolve. Thus, like job design, organization design is never finished. But this fact cannot discourage us from beginning the task; instead, it should encourage us to try new ideas and ways of working and relating — since change is inevitable, you might as well gain experience now and not worry about trying to create the perfect organization on the first attempt.

The boundary between job design and organization design is a fuzzy one. As job design begins to involve group work, you include some of the characteristics of organization design, because, indeed, you are designing a small organization. But, for our purposes, we will look at organization design from the perspective of the total organization, or, at least, the perspective of a large division. We will also look at issues that are beyond the scope of one manager to decide, because for managers it is important that they understand and try to influence all organization design decisions. This way they can ensure that these support the ends toward which they, themselves, are attempting to move the enterprise.

Structure as a Key Factor in Organizational Design

Organizational structure is a key component in creating organizational fit between goals, means and people. Currently, most organizations are structured in one of four ways. The first is according to the "Function" in an organization. If your organization has vice presidents (or their equivalent) of Marketing, Administration, Finance, Operations, and Human Resources (or some variation on these titles) reporting to a President, then your organization is likely functionally structured. Operations (or production) and the finance groups are probably the most powerful groups in the company. This structure is often found in companies that have found cost containment and management of the production function most crucial to their success.

The second way to organize is according to "Markets". In these organizations, the senior managers may have titles like VP Industrial Sales, and VP Consumer Sales, and these are the most powerful groups in the organization. This structure demonstrates the powerful influence of the various markets and the need to be able to sell to and respond to their individual requirements.

A variation on the market structure is the "Product" structure. Typically, consumer product companies are organized this way with vice presidents of, for example, Frozen Foods, Paper Products, and Laundry Products. Here, the consumer is again the dominant force, but the vehicle for sales may be the same for each product (e.g., the grocery store) and so it is the individual product, and often its advertising, which is responsible for success.

Finally, organizations which are very spread out geographically may be organized by "Regional". Here the key to success is seen as understanding the differences among the regions, either because of consumer differences or supplier differences. Senior people will have titles like V.P. Western Region, Eastern Region, etc.

Of course, it is never quite that simple. In the largest companies, there are usually various levels which are organized differently. A worldwide company may be structured by regions at the highest level, by products within a region, and functionally within a product organization.

The important point is that the choice of structure is based on the judgment of which emphasis — production, product, market or regional differences — is most crucial to the success of the organization. This judgment is generally based on historical factors, so we must look at how the changes that are coming will affect the choice of structure.

It is not at all clear which structure will be the most effective in the future. No doubt, all will have their place. But we can see that the criteria for choosing a structure will force changes. For example, for an organization that is servicing a very spread out market, in the past the regional structure may have been most appropriate. The electronic communications that are now available through the use of integrated office systems may make this structure unnecessary. This is happening in companies which formerly required regional billing centers. With new electronic cash registers it is possible to collect and analyze regional billing data at one central location.

The Special Case of Matrix Organizations

There is an interesting alternative to the four structures discussed above. In studies of organizations which seem to be successful in their markets and use the new technologies to good advantage, a number have been found to use the "matrix" structure to create a good fit between goals, means and people. In a matrix organization, each person reports to two superiors: the person in charge of the particular project or product on which the employee is working and the person in charge of the specialty area which the employee represents. For example, in a high tech product company, a software design specialist will report to both the manager of the product on which the specialist is working and the manager of software for the organization.

The structure is a complex one and difficult to handle. When it works well, the organization is very responsive and able to handle quality and productivity requirements very well. It seems to work best when the employees and management are well educated and professionally oriented. The qualities that make matrix work are also those which are found in entreprenurial, smaller companies. It may be that those large organizations which are able to successfully use the matrix structure are best able to retain those employees who are dissatisfied by the more traditional, bureaucratic organizational structures. But we do not know this yet. Many companies move to a matrix structure as a transitional phase between being functionally organized and later being product/market structured.

Integrated office systems offer one response to a major hurdle for the matrix organized company. That hurdle is ensuring that each person has the information needed to do the job. Because there are two bosses, it is very easy for each to assume that the other will pass on information, or for the employee to inform one boss of something that both need to know. The lack of information may result in missed deadlines or increased project costs. This, then, can lead to blame laying and to the major conflicts within and between the teams. Integrated office system — through electronic mail and computer conferencing — may assist in ensuring that each person is given the same information without returning to the less responsive bureaucratic mode of documenting everything through multiple memos and frequent face-to-face meetings.

Outside Options Available May Influence Organizational Design Decisions

Currently, many small firms do contract work for large organizations. But for the most part, the immediate client is the internal person responsible for that function, such as the marketing manager contracting for work from a market research firm. The small firm depends on the client to provide a great number of services: office space, administrative support, and most importantly, internal staff to interpret their mandate. In essence, the internal professional support group contracts for help from an external professional support group.

In the organization operating in the new environment described in Part One, it will often make sense to remove whole functions from the organization and to contract out the work. In this case, the external professional support group will be providing help to the line management, not another staff group. In effect, the external group *becomes* the staff function for the entire organization.

This significantly changes the structure of the enterprise and creates new demands for each side. The "outsiders" no longer have an internal staff to manage the contract and provide interpretation and implementation skills. No longer are they working with other professionals who share the same jargon and who know how to take the recommendations or proposals and make them effective. In the past, this internal staff group acted as a buffer between the contract people and the line management, interpreting the goals and style of the organization to the outside contractor and judging the suitability of any output of the external group for their specific organization. Now, the consultants must learn to translate their skills and expertise into products and proposals that can be clearly understood and used by the core management and employees of the large organization.

Additionally, there is a new load placed on the line management of the large organization. They must be able to quickly and coherently communicate the organization's goals, directions, culture and needs to outsiders. Although untrained in the profession of the particular consultant, they must become able to evaluate that person's work and learn how to apply it.

Another aspect of this phenomenon will be the use of contract labor in many positions in the company. They will be, in effect, "inside consultants", who will need to be managed much as the outside contract people must. They must have the same information communicated quickly and coherently to them and must be able to be utilized effectively from the first week of work. As they will be coming and going over the course of time, the organization must develop ways to capture anything they have learned that will be of use to future employees, such as why certain decisions were made, who to go to for particular kinds of information and why particular options will not work in this organization. This is referred to as building an "organizational history" and its development is facilitated by the existence of integrated office systems. This can begin to take the place of "Old Charlie" who used to work with incoming managers and show them the ropes. And that is important to the enterprise because "Old Charlie" now works for a consulting firm!

The organizational history — which is not a book, but rather a more informal information base within the company — helps the line managers make sure that all "newcomers" have consistent information about what is appropriate for that particular organization, and helps them become familiar with the way things are done. And, over time, the history will allow the organization to understand the impact of various decisions and the interrelationships between changes in goals, means, and people. For example, to learn about a particular policy decision, the working papers and minutes of meetings in which they were discussed provide vital clues as to what is the intent and purpose of the policy and what options were rejected.

The organizational history is only one example of the new devices that will be used to deal with the opportunities and problems that emerge during the structural change to "Lean and Mean". In general, all managers will need to become more knowledgeable in the areas of designing organizational structures and systems to support both the growing interdependence among organizations and the fluidity with which people move in and out of organizations. The insularity which previously characterized companies will not be appropriate anymore.

Distribution of Power is an Issue that Must Be Addressed

The introduction of integrated office systems invariably forces managers to face the issue of who controls information. The possibility of electronic access to files raises questions of who will be allowed access to them. In most organizations, the policy regarding the availability of files has evolved over time and the relationship between power and the availability of information has not been directly addressed in many years, if ever.

Organizational design involves, among other things, making decisions regarding who will have power to make decisions which commit organizational resources. These may be decisions to make loans, to purchase new equipment, to reward the performance of others, to accept a new client or develop a new product. Each of these decisions will be based on information available in the corporate database. Therefore, denying access to certain portions of this database is, in effect, a way to eliminate a person or group from the decisionmaking process.

When information did not move at the speed of light, management had to depend on the person on the front line or had to delay decisionmaking while awaiting information. Organizations were designed to support one of these ways of working. Often, front line supervisors and managers were given decision ceilings — all expenditures or loans below a certain level they could decide, any above must be referred upward for action.

The introduction of new technology forces a rethinking of these rules and the designs in place to support them. One option is to increase centralization of decisionmaking. Because much information is quickly available and easily analyzed, managers no longer need to be "close to the action" to assess risk and commit resources. This option decreases the responsibility of those people who work in the branches and enhances the responsibility and power of corporate headquarters personnel.

The alternative, of course, is to decentralize decisionmaking. Because information from the field can be so quickly integrated into the corporate database, the field people can perform the same analysis and have access to the same tools and perspectives as those at headquarters. Therefore, their decision ceiling can be increased without threat to the organization. This approach increases the power and responsibility of the personnel in the field and decreases that of corporate headquarters people.

Each of these approaches can, and has, been taken. Depending on your mission and goals, either can be appropriate. But, in general, organizations designing for the future will try to push responsibility and power further down in the organization to support and encourage responsible risk-taking and to demonstrate trust in their people. One fundamental rule is that

responsiblity and authority should be vested in the same person.

Thus, if you want a manager to be responsible for a market area, she or he should have authority for making decisions regarding that area. During the performance evaluation period the wisdom of decisions made can be reviewed and rewarded or punished as appropriate. But, in this now-constantly-changing environment, no one at corporate headquarters will likely be more in tune with the new demands and how to meet them. Any information available will be available corporate-wide, so access will no longer be a criteria in deciding who should make decisions.

We need to make the distinction between decentralization and pseudo-decentralization. In the latter, there is much talk about how management is pushing decisionmaking down in the organization in order to encourage entrepreneurial behavior and risk-taking. Yet, in actual behavior, senior management retains tight control and monitors decisions closely. Rather than waiting to see the results of decisions and thus trusting lower level managers, they intervene in unpopular or unusual decisions before the results can be seen. Under this scenario, managers quickly learn that they are not really trusted and will take very few risks. Status quo behavior is continued and little changes.

Although the new technology allows for the free flow of information, in these situations you will find that some is withheld. Rather than be second-guessed by their superiors, managers will enter incomplete information and, when decisions made at headquarters are wrong, will use these occasions to demonstrate how much better field decisions would have been. This is unhealthy behavior for the organization, but rational behavior from the perspective of the person who is being undermined. Pseudo-decentralization will often lead to this result. As in the case of allowing employees to help decide which performance data will be used, you will find that complete and timely information comes when those who are providing it understand how it will be used by others and have a role in setting up the systems for its collection.

Management is now faced with reassessing how well the structure of the organization supports the fit between the goals, means and people in the organization. Each of these is affected by changes that we have discussed: goals may change as a result of the changing market demands, means of reaching goals now include new office technologies, and the people on which the organization depends have changed both in terms of demographic characteristics and values. Each of these is an important factor to consider when contemplating the introduction of any change in an organization. A focus on organizational design, and how well it complements other changes contemplated, is always well advised.

THE KEY HUMAN RESOURCE ISSUES
Training, Retaining, Selecting, Inspecting and Protecting

4

Educating the Organization

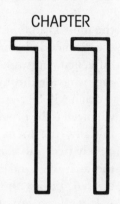

Managing the impact of new technology on people is not limited to dealing with the specific issues of job, office and organization design. Each line and staff manager must also be concerned with broader matters sometimes referred to as "Human Resource Issues". Each must be very aware of the organization's corporate-wide human resource policies and must focus a good deal of attention on managing the human side of the business. Again, this is the aspect of management which is the least likely to be overtaken by computer-based technologies.

While each manager should take on some responsibility for developing his or her employees — and most do concern themselves with health and safety and career planning issues — there remain many questions that cannot be dealt with by the individual manager alone. In this section we will look at several areas where corporate-wide action is required.

Education vs. Training

As senior management begins to appreciate the new demands placed upon the organization by the environment and employees, they will quickly see that the skills and attitudes needed to succeed in the this new world are unevenly distributed through the workforce. The need for an integrated plan to deal with this issue will become acute. Before any "training needs analysis" program is put in place, however, it is necessary to distinguish between the educational needs of the entire organization and particular training needs of the individuals within it.

In other words, there is a difference between developing a particular approach to work and to working — that is, education to encourage attitudes of flexibility, collegiality, adaptability, cooperation and collaboration — and learning the individual skills needed to support the attitudes — training for skills such as resolving conflict in the work group, using

137

the tools available, and providing non-directive leadership. If you like, the distinction is that education is an attempt to change behavior through influencing attitudes and knowledge, while training is more direct, changing behavior through teaching new skills.

Each will be required to ease the transition and both types of learning will need to be provided simultaneously in many organizations. However, initially, the focus must be on developing an education plan that is closely tied into the strategic plans for the organization. Only then will the attitudes and behaviors that support movement in the directions desired, in fact, be created and supported in the organization.

It is all too easy to get wrapped up in training for the new equipment. And, indeed, this training will be a vital and costly part of any success. But you must also remember that some of the larger issues that emerge during times of change can also be addressed, in part at least, by an educational approach. This aspect of learning needs to have sufficient time and money budgeted for it as well.

We have noted throughout this book how interrelated all the systems of an organization are. The technological, managerial and social systems are fitted together so that a change in one always requires that the others adapt to reestablish an equilibrium. A good education plan takes into account this need to get all the parts of the systems back into sync. It may include actions that focus attention on those systems which will need to be redesigned to support the implementation plans. These might include changing reward systems to support risk-taking and group productivity or selection systems to ensure that employees with the attitudes desired in the future are chosen now.

Furthermore, education of the people affected is required if the changes are to be effective and productivity and satisfaction increased. As well, to even understand the nature of the changes coming and how the organization will cope with them requires some education in many companies. Books, like this one, and conferences, seminars, presentations, and other educational forums can be used to help senior and middle management create the organizations they know will be most effective now and in the future.

Training will be a major component of any plan to introduce an organization-wide change such as the introduction of new technology. While seldom ignored, too often training is left to the vendor of the equipment and fails to meet the many needs and larger issues faced by the company.

One major issue to be addressed in connection with training is, who will be part of the new organization and who will not? What are the organizational responsibilities for employees who will no longer be required? In many organizations, no one will need to leave even though some jobs may be eliminated, because there are other tasks to be done and the people can be retrained to do them. But we must face the reality that in some instances, some people will no longer be needed. If this issue is ignored or minimized, then the morale in the company is usually lowered and it is not uncommon to see resistance to the introduction of technology as a result. Facing the issue is painful, but necessary. (One policy that can be developed is that those who will not be needed will be trained in new skills so that they will be employable in the future, even if not at this location. We will return to this subject in greater detail later.)

The first step is to develop policies regarding the organization's responsibilities for the people affected by the changes. For example, as the organization chooses to become more flexible and seeks new ways to encourage this, it must then analyze all the jobs and tasks to see how to make them supportive of its goal. Often, integrated office systems are discovered to be an important support tool for realizing the goal of increased flexibility. In most instances, there will be some tasks that are better done by a computer-based system and there are some jobs that will no longer be required at all, becoming redundant. Part of the education strategy would be to ensure that there are policies in place throughout the organization regarding how the new tasks will be combined into jobs and what will be done for the people whose current jobs are eliminated. These policies need to be communicated and care must be taken to ensure that each person responsible for implementing the policies understands their purpose and how to apply them.

In some organizations, it is reasonable to retrain some employees and let the redundancy be taken care of through voluntary resignation and retirement. For some, this is not an option. To be competitive and be able to offer jobs to any they must let some go. Fair enough. But there should be some humane policies regarding these people. Two weeks' notice and a thank you is just not enough.

The challenge of dealing with those people whose jobs may disappear should be a very real concern to the organization. It is also not one for which a specific set of guidelines can be defined. Rather, it reflects the very character of the organization. It is through the actions with respect to these people that the organizational values will be judged.

As every person will need some degree of computer literacy and skills, in every organization, it is not too much to expect that even those who must be let go might be given a general introductory training course that would allow them to compete in the job market. The aim of such courses should be to increase the individual's ability to adapt to change, to understand how the computer may affect the way we work and, to use computer-based technologies in everyday life.

Note that computer programming is not included — every prediction indicates that programming will become an esoteric skill used only by a few and that computing will become easier, requiring little, if any, programming.

However, you may argue, if these people could learn these skills mentioned, they would not be redundant. But that is not quite right. It is entirely possible to have perfectly capable people whom the organization just cannot absorb. And it is conceivable that some people who are not top performers can still learn the skills needed in the future. They may be performing at less than their best in the particular organization for reasons totally unrelated to technology.

While the initial reaction to this suggestion of training for those who have been declared redundant may be one of disbelief, it is not as unlikely as you may think. Already, there have been several instances of this kind of training being guaranteed to workers through the collective bargaining agreement. One such example was the agreement between the old American Telephone and Telegraph Company and its twenty-two local unions in the U.S. In Japan, Sumitomo Metal Industries trains excess employees in computer and related skills. In Canada, an insurance company which has identified a number of areas where layoffs will occur in the next few years has given employees up to two years' notice and has offered to train each employee in job skills before they leave. It is a more sensible and honest solution to the issue of redundancy than promising there will be "no layoff due to new technology" and then blaming subsequent layoffs on the "recession" or other reasons.

The Training Challenge

How do you plan for training of those whose jobs are changing and the retraining of those whose jobs will, in fact, disappear? This training challenge will need to be met through the development of well-timed, innovative and continuous programs.

One of the most common errors made is to misunderstand the concept of "cost-efficiency" as it applies to training. To take a rather simple example, when organizations begin to use word processors they often attempt to train as many potential operators as is possible at one time. This appears to be an efficient use of the training provided by the vendor.

But this efficiency may reduce effectiveness in the long run. All too often the trained people do not have access to machines on a regular basis because availability was not"justified" for all of them. Rather, it was hoped that they would create demand for the equipment or provide a pool from which substitute labor could be drawn.

Paradoxically, this training "efficiency" results in overall costs to the organization. When trained people can not use the equipment regularly, they quickly lose the skills acquired in the short training course. Then, when the equipment is available, additional training is not provided because there is the assumption that they are already trained. Consequently, the equipment is not used to its fullest potential, because more experienced operators often end up doing on-the-job training of their colleagues anyway — time for which the organization pays in addition to that which was orginally spent in training and not put into use — and, most importantly, the people experience a great deal of stress, frustration and anger.

These costs to the organization are rarely documented but are nonetheless real and not inconsequential. In many instances, one-on-one or very small group training will prove to be less costly in the long run for the organization that wishes to gain the promised benefits from its rather large capital expenditure. The realization that the introduction of new technology is an ongoing process should result in a commitment to provide ongoing training. As new uses for the technology are discovered, as new processes and ways of working emerge, as new capabilities are introduced, and as people move through the organization, training will be needed to satisfy emerging needs. An active approach to planning for training, and the development of training processes which allow for a flexible approach, will both be required.

In addition, organizations should try their best to retain good performers whose jobs may have disappeared and to retrain them in needed skills. This benefits the organization in several ways. It continues to have access to the experience, loyalty and productivity of good workers. It gains the loyalty and respect of other workers who see positive organizational values in action. Moreover, it warns poor performers to shape up.

The rate of change is increasing and with it the rate of obsolesence of old jobs and the emergence of new ones. The organization is well advised to develop skills in retraining employees, because this will be an ongoing need in the future organization. The people who can change and adapt are just the people who can be retrained most easily. Organizations must aim to attract a core of people who can meet the corporate needs, and then must protect these people against the ravages that time and change may inflict on their particular jobs.

No one knows, for sure, what the jobs of the future will be. We can not train in specific skills and feel confident that there will be employment in those areas over the long term. Therefore, the first "skill" needed is really an attitude. Openness to change and the ability and willingness to continue learning throughout one's life will be a valued skill in every employee. This attitude can be taught, provided the right setting is available. It is difficult to teach under duress.

The ability to benefit from retraining is not directly related to age or level in the organization. There are some supervisors or managers who will say "All this is fine for others, but my people can't cope with the demands of retraining." Nonsense! You would be amazed what people can learn when they have a supportive environment and when they understand and support the need to learn. The adage that "you can't teach an old dog new tricks" applies only to old dogs. People never lose their ability to learn. What is lacking usually is an appropriate setting.

If you doubt this, consider for a moment what happens when a grandparent goes to visit a grandchild these days. In order to play with the child, the first thing the grandparent must do is learn to use the newest video game that the child has. And the grandparent usually does learn. So the grandparent is indeed capable of learning to use new (computer-based) skills. The only difference is that in this setting she or he was not threatened with the loss of esteem, and possibly employment, that so often accompanies the skill training that takes place in an organizational setting.

The stereotype that many people cannot be trained to use the new equipment comes, in part, from allowing equipment manufacturers to control the training process. Just as many of them have designed user-friendly equipment that is only friendly to computer-literate people, so have they designed training programs that are appropriate only to those who already know how to use the new technology. One employee describes the training experience on computerized long-distance telephone equipment this way:

> The training, in terms of teaching the employee that the machine knows everything, and that the employee knows nothing, was absolutely amazing. I never saw anything like it. The operator was taught to operate the technology by basically a tape recorder — a magnetic tape (attached to an operating) position, which instructed her to do certain things — at which time the tape would stop. And she would have to figure out what she was supposed to do next. ... if she was unable to determine what to do, the tape would never move, it would simply stop. Or, alternatively, if you made an error and keyed something incorrectly, you would get a very piercing noise in your ear and an

error message would print up on your video display terminal. And you would have to continue to key until you hit the right button, and each time you keyed an incorrect button, you would receive this piercing tone in your ear ... the effect on an individual is just devastating, because you're wondering — How many errors did everybody else make? Am I stupid? The ultimate, of course, is that the machine knows everything.[6]

Any training programs introduced into an organization must meet the criteria for selection of tools set out by senior management or the task force. That is, just as hardware and software that does not assume employees are mature and competent human beings is not acceptable, training programs that create feelings such as described here should be unacceptable.

While the case of the operator training was a dramatic example, more subtle forms of harrassment and dehumanization are often built into training materials and programs that are used at all levels of the organization. Any training program that would be seen as insulting or inappropriate for senior managers should certainly be suspected of being inadequate for any employee. And I doubt many managers would sit still for any program that required them to experience a shrill piercing noise when they made an error. A good rule of thumb would be that a program under consideration should be pretested on the people one and two levels above those who will have to undergo it, and under the same conditions. I suspect that many of the badly designed training courses would never be approved if they had been subjected to this test.

Training, of course, will not be limited to skill training for equipment use. It is clear that training will be an important component of any job redesign effort. When there are new tasks to be performed, new ways to do these tasks, and new tools to help, people will need to be taught how. When work is changed from an individual to group basis, there are many new skills to learn such as working in a group, how to manage work, how to manage conflict within the group, and the like.

There are many options that can be considered for training. In terms of sources of training, there are computer "institutes" emerging in every city, many resorts now offer computer camps, established training programs offer skill training in many of the areas cited above, universities and colleges offer night and weekend training in addition to the more traditional programs, and many organizations will provide in-house seminars on any relevant topic. Methods of training now include video and computer-based systems in addition to the more traditional approaches.

The training of different levels in the organization is also a factor. While all training should respect the dignity and maturity of each employee, it is a fact that at each level, different degrees of availability and "need to know" will prevail. For example, at the most senior levels, executives will need to understand both how to use particular kinds of technology as well as understand the implications of decisions they may make with respect to the applications of technology within their respective departments. The education and training vehicles designed for them would be different from those designed for individuals who did not have the "implications" piece to consider.

Each organization will need to decide for itself which options are most important to support its particular change efforts. The expenses will be considerable and effectiveness will be a vital concern.

The demands on the training function will be heavy. Some companies are already well organized in this area. For others, it will mean increasing the training staff or contracting out large amounts of the training or a combination of these. In all, it is important that the senior management require careful coordination between the education plan, training plans and the business plan. And they must also require constant evaluation of the impact of training interventions to ensure that the criteria and guidelines set out for successful implementation are adhered to in this vital area.

The Changing Nature of Work and Careers

We have managed change for many years. But usually the changes have come gradually and the effects on other parts of the organization have seemed to come one at a time so that they could be dealt with within the course of normal and routine management.

Integrated office systems, the new worker and the new environment have combined to force us to change much more quickly. The introduction of new technology quickly affects every part of the organization. No where is this more visible than when we look at the changing nature of work and how it affects such Human Resource issues as career planning, performance appraisal, alternative work patterns, and the relationship of these to affirmative action programs. We have already seen that training is fundamental to the successful introduction of new technology; other parts of the Human Resources system are also involved to a large extent.

Career Planning

The concept of a planned career has only taken meaning in most organizations in the last decade or two. Prior to that, movement within a company was mainly aimed at filling the company's needs for certain skills in certain areas. People were expected to take what was offered and to trust that they would be looked after. With the emergence of both larger, more complex organizations, and individuals who seek more control over their own futures, career management has emerged.

Most often this activity has been aimed at people destined for management positions, but in some more progressive organizations, system-wide career planning for all personnel is the norm. In reality, though, for most of the blue, pink and white collar workers who will probably never move into management positions, this planning has been more "job" and "skill acquisition" planning than the planning of actual moves within the company. But, nonetheless, this represents quite a change from the past.

New technology is one of the forces which is altering the career planning process. Most of traditional career planning procedures involve looking at how successful people have progressed through the company and using their experiences as a model. It is not quite this simple, of course, but the point is that the past has been a useful reference for the planning process. For example, many companies move management trainees through a set of positions according to guidelines which reflect the patterns followed by other managers who were judged high performers.

We now know that many of the jobs which exist today will not exist in ten or twenty years and that the jobs that remain may be so different that we cannot predict the skills that will be required. In addition, new jobs will emerge which must be filled, and we do not know what skills and abilities will be required for these either. To say this presents a dilemma to the indivdual who is trying to plan a career is an understatment. To give an example from the past, when computers first appeared, they were predicted to be of limited use to the average business and nobody predicted that within a few years there would be a massive need for computer programmers, keypunch operators, systems managers, maintenance people and other related personnel. Our ability to predict the skills needed in the future is limited by our ability to imagine which discoveries will create new industries and which will be of limited importance. (At one point, before the telephone was patented, it was thought there would be a telegraph machine on each desk and that all people would need to know Morse code!)

The people in an organization responsible for ensuring that necessary skills are available when needed and that there is a pool of people from which to draw as opportunities arise are faced with a major challenge when new technology is being introduced. How will the plans they have made change? What contingency plans will need to be created or altered? Will the necessary skills be available from inside, or must they look outside? Questions such as these will immediately arise.

Additionally, for the individuals who are concerned about managing their own careers, a number of questions will come up. When implementation is first occurring, most people concentrate on "staying alive". They concentrate on learning to use the equipment, understanding how it changes the way they work or how they can use it to alter the way they work, and on getting used to a new set of relationships.

But later, when things have calmed down, they will begin to ask: Where can I go from here? What training will I need to keep on the career path I was on before? Is the career path I was on before still a viable one? What new paths have opened up that I might want to consider?

To deal with these questions, planners will need to know how the organization is evolving as a result of the new opportunities and abilities that new technologies create. But, even more important is that everyone within the organization learns to accept the fact that ambiguity and uncertainty are the *price* of flexibility and increased responsiveness. The demand for structured or completely predictable career paths will have to be reduced. Individuals will need to learn that it is impossible to promise what the next move might be, let alone one five years from now.

One of the biggest changes from both the organization and individual perspective will be the increasing experience of multiple careers. That is, for most people, the career for which they are originally trained and in which they have their first work experiences will rarely be the career from which they retire. It is increasingly common to have whole career streams disappear, and it is also common for individuals to realize, in their thirties or forties, that they are no longer satisfied by their career and wish a major change. We have all seen examples of this: lawyers who become musicians, hairdressers who become salesmen, social workers who become doctors and teachers who take up marina management. The difference is that in the future it will be expected.

Along the way, however, we need to develop attitudes that support the acceptance of such change. In many instances, it will require returning to school and all that that implies: a reduced standard of living perhaps, reduced power and status in society, and the loss of a formerly valued skill upon which one could depend for making a living. And increasingly we will have no choice in the matter, making the strains even greater.

You shouldn't, however, assume that career planning will be abandoned. Rather, our definition of the process is what is changing. The focus is moving from plotting specific paths and developing skills specific to these jobs to discovering what the fundamental motivators are in each person and helping her or him learn to evaluate a job on the basis of whether it provides the motivation and developmental opportunities desired. Career development becomes the responsibility of an individual and may be less tied to the organization's plans. This fits nicely with the new employee's need for self-development and individual control; however, it can certainly play havoc with the organization's planning and staffing systems.

Within the organization, an increasingly sophisticated planning system will have to be developed, which is able to track the fundamental components of jobs and to match these to the most important attributes of the employee. Then the job opportunities will need to be communicated to employees on the basis of how the job contributes to their long-term development. People will be less inclined to define themselves according to "functions" such as accounting, marketing and human resources. Rather, they will be able to define the characteristics of the ideal job and analyze each opportunity on the basis of these characteristics.

Working Patterns

As you can see from our discussion of the move to career development, people will have very different career experiences in the future. They will move in and out of the work force, and increasingly, the work or career they are in at the moment will reflect their stage in life and personal growth as much as anything else. The ability to work in new ways will include working at non-traditional times, in non-traditional places and sharing jobs in non-traditional ways.

There has been a considerable amount of news coverage about concepts variously called flexible work schedules, flexitime, alternative work patterns, work-sharing, flexiplace and so on. These all, in one way or another, refer to the increasingly common phenomenon of office workers working schedules other than nine to five, five days a week, or working at places other than the central office. In some instances, several of these characteristics are found in one job.

The earliest pattern to emerge was the desire to work different hours from "normal". Sometimes the desire was to avoid the traffic jams of rush hour, sometimes to be at home when the children got home from school, sometimes to be able to have "extra" days off for personal use, and sometimes as recognition that the demands of the job were quite variable and the individual was too busy some days and not busy enough on others. Alternative working schedules, whether individually set or organizationally agreed to, have become quite common in some industries.

A newer trend is that of working at alternative locations. These may either be the so-called "satellite" centers where several members of an organization work at an office closer to their home, or where one actually works in one's own home. A combination, in which the individual works some time in the office and some time at home, is also becoming more common.

Work-sharing is still newer and less is known about how it will evolve. Here the concept is that one or more persons share the tasks that have, up until now, been regarded by the organization as comprising one job. It can be a secretarial job where two people trade off days, a clerical job where one person works mornings and one afternoons, or even a research position in which a few people divide up the tasks and do the work associated with their part from home.

Obviously, it is possible to combine several of these concepts so that, as in the last example, you have a work sharing, flexitime, flexiplace arrangement. The combinations are many and growing.

What all of these have in common is that they are innovative approaches to work. They require that the representatives of the organization who are responsible for seeing that the particular work gets done be open to new ways of working and new ways of managing. In many instances, it also means creating new ways of evaluating work that is done, because old evaluation techniques were linked to more traditional work patterns. More on this below.

The new integrated systems are a major factor in creating the opportunity to try innovative work patterns. Through the use of telecommunications, working off-site is unnoticeable to those who deal with these workers. Through the use of shared files and electronic messaging, handing off responsibility for tasks, as in job sharing is greatly eased. Because so many of the emerging work tasks will be computer-based, it is clear that an ever-increasing variety of jobs could become candidates for the application of alternative work patterns.

The major benefits for individuals are control over one's own work life. Often there is increased independence, and there may be some financial gains such as reduced wardrobe and commuting costs. For the organization, there may be reduced support costs if the individual is working from home and doesn't need an office and increased productivity due to a better matching of availability and task demands.

But it isn't all roses. The individual working from home or in a part-time arrangement may be out of the communication network necessary for keeping in touch with the organization and may also experience social isolation. The key to success in managing these new workers is in the understanding of what the impact of changing work patterns will be on each individual involved. Care must be taken to ensure that individuals are not forced out of the organizational mainstream and that new ways to meet their social and growth needs are included in any change. Positive experiences to date have in many instances been based on employee initiative and voluntary change. Financial pressures in the future, however, may tempt managers to try to force such changes onto nonvolunteers.

Some companies, in looking at the cost savings in having people work from home, have tried to impose such changes. For the most part, these efforts have been unsuccessful. Dissatisfaction, turnover and reduced productivity have resulted. After all, people work for a variety of reasons and the social contact and the feeling of being part of an organization is a powerful force for many. So the introduction of alternative work patterns must not derive from unrealistic expectations about cost savings.

One high tech company was growing more quickly than could be accomodated by the available office space. So engineers and programmers were given computers to work with in their homes. To try to overcome the problem of isolation, each person was expected to work half of the work day in a (shared) office. But no one was given the opportunity to choose who worked from home or when. Schedules were set and each person worked at home either each morning or each afternoon. This "solution" pleased no one and the experiment had to be abandoned in a short time. For one reason, people were now commuting the same distance in order to have half the amount of office time. Work begun at the office or at home had to be interrupted to shift location based on the clock, not on logical breaks. Each person only saw half of the group, so communications were a problem despite the attendance requirement. All in all, it was not an effective solution to the problem.

However, sensitively approached, an organization *can* introduce alternative patterns that will benefit the employee and still realize gains. Recent research has been focusing on which types of employees are most successful at working from home and which types of tasks are best. This can help guide the choices. Contrary to the fears expressed that "homework" would be of the low skill, low involvement variety, the most successful attempts are built on whole tasks on which a person can work independently and thoughtfully, such as writing or analyzing. Successful candidates are independent people who do not have a large number of social contacts at work and who value solitude.

Performance Appraisal

Alternative work patterns can compound the difficulties already raised in our discussion of job design. Performance ratings are often tied to the quality and, if appropriate, quantity of output. But when employees are using the new technologies, you have little of the old information on which to base a performance rating. These people may, as noted, be working from their homes or other, off-site locations. They may be working any variety of hours which do not always overlap with those of the "rater". And, of course, the output of the labor itself may be difficult to define or appraise.

To deal with this issue, it is imperative that new criteria for performance evaluation be developed. For the reasons we discussed in the Participation section of Chapter Seven, these will need to be created in consultation with the people who will be judged by them. Also, the methods of collecting the data used to judge performance needs to be similarly decided.

For example, traditionally we have been able to distinguish good work from bad work on a variety of bases. For typists, it may be the appearance of letters and documents and the number of pages typed. Criteria has included the skill that the typist exercises in correcting errors in submitted documents, as, for example, when a typist is asked to send out a letter "after you're happy with it". If then, the letter that goes out has a major grammatical error or is badly laid out, the typist is judged less than competent.

With integrated office systems, these criteria will be less useful. In the first place, many people will compose and send their own letters. But even when a support staff person is doing it for another, the system will provide spelling and grammar checks and will perform the layout function. All letters and documents will look the same because the computer provides the "standard" format into which the words get typed. What then is the basis for performance appraisal? The support staff certainly recognize the problem. Comments such as "You can't identify who did what" and "I've lost my pride in product because you can't distinguish good from bad" are not uncommon.

Of course, it is not only a problem for support staff. Judging the performance of a professional, even in today's office environment, is a difficult problem. Many of the implicit criteria used are based on appearances. Does the person look like he or she is working hard? How good are the presentations? What kind of hours are being kept? These are common but unstated bases of appraisal.

In the future, people will likely be working in locations that management can not monitor. With information going directly to senior management, there will be fewer opportunities for presentations. What, then, are the new judgment criteria? The natural inclination is to measure what you can measure — such things as number of hours signed-on the machine (as a substitute for how many hours she or he is in the office) and the appearance of memos and other documents. But it is clear that these are not valid for judging how adequate and appropriate the person's contribution has been.

One rule of appraisal is, to put it bluntly,

You get what you measure.

Therefore, if you measure number of hours signed-on the machine, the number of hours signed-on will increase dramatically. If you measure lines of type output, you will see this increase, even if the lines output are merely repeats of what was put out last hour. A phone company learned this sad truth when it put in a computer-based system for its operators and began measuring their "productivity" based on how long it took each to handle a call. As one operator reported

> ... they take you off the board and they talk to you, and they have reams and reams of computer sheets.... And it tells them how many calls you've taken, how long you took ... So it's straining ... (Your manager will) say "Look, you're pulling my group results down ... you've got to work faster". So we get customers calling back saying "Why did the person disconnect me?" Well, they're worried about their (average), they're worried about management leaning over their shoulder saying "Go faster." That's why people are getting cut off, that's why they're getting wrong numbers.[7]

Because the choice was made to measure speed, speed is what they got. Of course, this is not effectiveness. Measures of such things as number of calls successfully completed and customer satisfaction are probably more relevant. But the computer, *as programmed*, could not evaluate those.

In general, performance criteria must be derived from and linked to the basic goals of the organization. If, during a change, management is trying to increase the amount of behavior that we have called innovative, flexible and collegial, then measures of this kind of performance must be gathered. While these measures are much more difficult to collect and evaluate, it is possible. And the effort must be made or the performance appraisal system will eventually be a major block to the attainment of fundamental organizational goals.

Impact on Affirmative Action Plans

A natural outcome of changing career patterns, new appraisal systems and, most significantly, alternative work patterns, is the ability to include in the workforce those individuals who desire to work but have not been able to meet the traditional demands of the office setting. These people often include the disabled, disadvantaged, and women who have child care responsibilities which preclude traditional working arrangements.

The introduction of integrated office technologies can, then, provide an opportunity to expand employment of targeted groups and help the organization meet Affirmative Action goals. Again, as always, it is a matter of how it is handled. The technologies merely provide the opportunity. Managers must be innovative in their applications to turn these opportunities into realities. One government agency has added the capability to turn screen-based information into voice information so that blind workers can respond to callers' questions regarding the processing of their claims. The blind worker hears what the person with vision sees on the screen and interprets this information for the caller. This agency now has a larger pool of employees to draw from and the blind people now have new opportunities to work and gain financial independence.

One fear often expressed is that the new technologies will create new "job ghettos" and that the organizations will take advantage of minorities. This is certainly a possibility if, for example, low skill, piece-rate tasks are created and moved into homes of parttime workers who are not covered by benefits and whose working conditions are not monitored.

Some have expressed the (in my mind, ill-advised) hope that working at home will relieve the pressure to create day-care facilities because the mother will be able to watch the children while she works. One dictation equipment manufacturer actually had an ad in a business magazine which showed a women using the equipment while the child stared at her from a playpen. Clearly, neither the person who designed the ad, nor those who approved have ever tried to combine the use of dictation equipment and fulltime child care. They never would have tried to indicate that the tasks can be mixed.

While we may talk of "cottage industries" very positively when we look at all of the high technology applications that have sprung up — such as software design and the development of new computer systems in a person's garage — we fail to remember that in the original cottage industries very poor people were weaving cloth at home for very low wages under hideous conditions. (Of course, the factories that wiped out the cottage industries did not exactly meet what we would now consider to be acceptable standards either.)

On a more positive note, the use of integrated office systems can increase the opportunity to employ the handicapped in the office as well. Electronic mail reduces the need for a telephone and thus a deaf person may be able to be employed more fully. Many physically handicapped can use a keyboard to retrieve files when they would have difficulty accessing filing cabinets. The reduced need for travel that the new technologies creates can, as well, be a boon to those who are bedridden. For those with a speech impediment, communicating via a terminal means that the need to talk is greatly reduced. And there will be some jobs that are created that are not challenging for most, but are quite fulfilling for the mentally handicapped. And for those who choose to work from home and have the resources to do it, the "cottage" can be the ultimate participant-designed work environment. The choice is there for those who choose to make it.

There is no "technological imperative" concerning the new technologies. The use, for good or ill, is always in the hands of those who administer, design, and most importantly, evaluate the impact of the systems. If these people use design criteria that support the evolution of the organization toward its goals, then the technology will be used in a coherent, consistent manner. And if these goals include developing and maintaining a work environment in which people thrive and grow to develop new capacities for their own good and the good of the company, then these systems will be of benefit. The onus is always on management to perform its fundamental function of creating the vision, communicating it, and monitoring the progress toward it.

Are Offices Safe Anymore?

Humans are interesting beings. The mind and body are so interrelated that what affects one immediately and profoundly affects the other. So we must spend some time looking at the mental and physical effect of using integrated office systems and their components.

There is a whole science involved in studying the impact of machines on people, called ergonomics. This study involves understanding the physiology of eyes, muscles and skeleton. It also is concerned with the way in which people gather information, read displays, react to light and dark, and similar psychological phenomena. Through this study, great gains have been made in the design of the equipment to mitigate many of the symptoms found in the early use of it.

This is not to say that the symptoms are no longer experienced. Indeed, there are few introduction efforts of any sort in which no one feels any physical strain. Because each person is different and works in ways slightly different from the theoretical model, each must learn how to personalize the technology so that it fits the workstyle. And, for some it may mean compromising on particular aspects of the use of the equipment.

The best design in the world will not overcome stress and fear, which are normal outcomes of any implementation of new technology. It comes from having to learn new methods and being unsure of the consequences of making a mistake and of not knowing how to correct errors. It is exacerbated when employees do not know if their jobs are to be eliminated, when they do not know how the organization will treat those whose jobs become redundant, when they do not participate in the decision process or design process and yet must implement decisions, and when they work in jobs which do not have a sufficient level of motivation.

Any or all of these situations are found in many present-day office change efforts. Moreover, there is a high correlation between mental stress and the experience of physical symptoms. Stress causes the clenching of muscles, which can lead to pain. Stress also causes headaches, increased blood pressure, fatigue, loss of concentration, and various other ailments.

Many people recognize the relationship between what they are feeling mentally and their physical state. However, in most traditional organizations, it is not "normal" for people to complain about the design of their jobs or the insecurity they are feeling regarding their careers. To discuss one's fears and insecurities is to introduce a level of "personal intimacy" that is not usually found in the organization. The fact that these fears and insecurities are job-related is not considered relevant.

Therefore, we see that people complain about their physical aches and pains instead of discussing the mental strains that have caused the symptoms to appear. Too often, the response is to deal with the physical symptoms by trying to rearrange the physical space and furnishings. By ignoring the real cause, the organization is not likely to resolve the problem. And it might waste a lot of money trying.

A second possible response is to deny the reality of the symptoms. That is, someone from within the organization or a representative of the equipment vendor will try to convince the employees that they could not possibly be feeling those pains or symptoms, because the equipment is specifically designed to avoid them, or that the pains are unrelated to the technology. One word processing operator developed a rash when there was a major change in the equipment and its location. She said "When I complained to the manager about the rash, he said I was in menopause." This kind of response only aggravates the situation. Now, the employee, in addition to feeling stress, has been indirectly told that either he or she is "crazy" or the organization is lying about its willingness to deal with problems caused by the new technology. To believe either of these will surely increase the stress felt.

After employees find that complaining of physical symptoms is useless, discussion may disappear, giving management the feeling that they have dealt with the problems. But again, the real problems have not been solved. The usual result is that the employees will deal with their stresses and strains in other, less direct ways, such as being increasingly late or absent or by leaving the organization.

It is instructive to track the ebbing and waning of complaints about health and to relate this to the stage of implementation and the behavior of management. In the case presented above, this tracking was systematically done. In this instance, the employees had a great deal of input into decisionmaking during the initial introduction of a new office system. Previous to this, management had not usually asked employees for their opinions and this opportunity to participate was enthusiastically received.

A great deal of time and money was spent on the design of the physical space and furnishings. A new location was established, new furniture purchased and the technology decisions themselves were based, in large part, on the "humaneness" of the equipment. Unfortunately, the criteria for selection (its impact on the people) was not extended to other parts of the work environment. There were a number of factors that contributed to the problems experienced.

One factor of the project is that it was originally funded for one year and was due to be evaluated at the end of that year. Yet, when the year was up, the project was refunded and no final evaluation was done. This continued for two and a half years until the project was officially confirmed as an ongoing department.

The major problem was that management considered the change an "experiment", which was what led to involvement of employees in the first place. The participative approach taken was not a reflection of a change in style and management quickly went back its more traditional ways once the project was underway. Decisions regarding job redesign, assignment, work scheduling, and so on were no longer shared with the people involved.

In addition, the experimental nature of the project meant that the people in the project were given experimental job titles and temporary job classifications. In a government setting, this is a very insecure position in which to be. The employees did not know what would happen to them if the project were cancelled; their previous jobs no longer existed and yet they did not have permanent status in their current assignments. Due to the temporary nature of the project, they were not given performance appraisals for the first two years, and yet appraisals are the basis on which one competes for future jobs.

Throughout this project, information was collected from the employees as to their attitudes regarding their jobs, supervision, the physical environment and their health. During the initial stage they were pleased with the physical design, very upset about the job design, and expressed little concern about their health. They still were happy about the participative approach and looked at the problems as natural to an experimental situation.

Later, as the situation became more "normal" and more traditional, the sentiments changed. Management had made some effort to redesign the jobs to include more of the characteristics that the employees felt important. Though most of the employees were not directly involved in the redesign effort, some of the changes were clearly appropriate and positively received. On the other hand, there were numerous complaints about headaches and skin rashes, fear regarding radiation, and fatigue. The employees expressed concern for their futures as the "experiment" went beyond the one-year deadline without a confirmation of status, and they resented the lack of participation which they had had previously.

Finally, with the status confirmed and the employees in permanent job classifications, a final set of data was collected. This survey showed that the number of complaints about physical ailments had decreased markedly. Yet now the employees were engaging in acts of passive resistance and subtle sabotage. They were considerably less motivated to work hard and were very open about saying so. This last survey showed the results of management not having taken the complaints about physical symptoms seriously and that management behavior had not changed despite previous survey data which showed increasing stress levels.

This one example demonstrates many of the areas for concern regarding the physical impact of working with the new technology. Increasing stress levels led to an increase in physical symptoms that no amount of attention to the physical design could alleviate. Yet good attention to physical design had initially given management a starting point for the acceptance of the technology. When the problems which led to the symptoms were not dealt with, employees' behavior changed in subtle ways which had negative outcomes for the organization. In this instance, the employees were already unionized but the union was a weak one. In other cases, this situation could have lead to unionization attempts (in a non-union setting) or to job action by a strong union.

Specific VDT Related Concerns

There are three health issues often raised about the use of video display terminals (VDTs). These concerns are not related to the ability of the technology to adapt to the needs of individuals, rather the issues are based on fundamental aspects of VDTs. First, there are worries about the physical health consequences of working at VDTs. Second, there are concerns regarding the potential impact of ionizing and non-ionizing radiation possibly given off by the terminals. Finally, there are some disturbing reports regarding possible neurological impacts, similar to those found in studies of people watching television.

There is documented evidence that working at VDTs can cause some people to experience physical problems such as headaches, eyestrain, and pains in the neck, back, shoulders, wrists and legs. Common causes of the headaches and eyestrain are glare, flicker rate of the screen, brightness of the screen, the use of bifocals and stress. The pains are often the result of posture demands of the equipment, which cause the operator to sit in unnatural positions in order to avoid glare, to look through bifocals, to look back and forth from paper to screen, or similar physical exertions.

There has been a lot of attention paid to this area and vendors of equipment are working with furniture manufacturers to produce equipment and furnishings that are well designed and extremely adaptable to the individual's needs. Unfortunately, when budgeting for integrated office systems, the line item that tends to get reduced first is the new furniture. The tendency is to try to "get by" on the old furniture and the old interior design. While understandable, it is a false economy. Unhealthy working conditions are neither acceptable on a human basis nor useful to the organization, because they reduce productivity.

The second major area of concern is with the effect of potential radiation exposure from working with the VDTs. This is a highly controversial area. Numerous studies have demonstrated that VDTs do not emit a level of ionizing or non-ionizing radiation any higher than the background radiation in which we live. Yet there are so many stories circulated about higher rates of birth defects, miscarriages, and cataracts among people who work with VDTs, that the average user does not know what to believe. One wants to believe the studies, yet the consequences of being wrong are so profound. Therefore, many people are choosing to take precautions against the potential threat "just in case". Given that there is uncertainty within the scientific community regarding the long-term effects of continuous exposure to low level radiation (even if only a minute increment over what is received in the normal course of life), this conservative stance cannot be faulted.

However, it seems that some of the conservative approaches could do more damage to users, when one takes into account the psychological and physical implications of some of the responses. For example, in some offices, employees are actually given lead aprons to wear while working with VDTs. These are aprons similar to those put on patients when having X-rays done during a dental checkup. The intent is to protect the reproductive organs of the users from potentially harmful radiation. But there are a number of problems with this "solution". First of all, imagine the fatigue experienced by a terminal operator at the end of a day spent carrying a lead weight around the neck. Such a precaution would necessarily lead to an increase in the physical strain of the job. Secondly, consider the image created by working with these aprons. You would feel that you were in a war zone, constantly fighting off deadly rays. You would wonder if the apron is sufficient. And fear for the parts of your body that were not lead covered. Other people working in or visiting the area would worry about their safety and perhaps avoid the area. All of this must increase the mental strain of the job.

The total stress experienced by a worker is the sum of all the physical *and* psychological stress involved. In the previous instance, the solution must be considered inappropriate because the stress levels that it generates are likely to be higher than is healthy for day-to-day living.

Another typical response to the radiation concern is to transfer to other duties any employee who becomes pregnant and normally uses a VDT in the course of her work. This solution is not terribly useful in meeting the concerns voiced by most people who fear the VDT. If, in fact, VDTs do emit a level of radiation that has a harmful effect on the development of a fetus — which evidence to date has not shown to be the case — then the transfer comes too late. The fetus is most susceptible to damage during its first few days or weeks of life. For the vast majority of women, pregnancy is not confirmed until four to six weeks after conception. Therefore, by the time the transfer takes place, the potential damage, if any existed, would already have been done.

But other damage is done by this policy. By its very existence, the transfer policy gives credence to the stories linking birth defects with VDT use and, by extension, to other stories about the potentially damaging effect of working with them. Thus, employees are even more likely to fear for the safety of their unborn children and for their own safety. This, by definition, will increase the mental stress level of the office, which will lead, in turn, to increases in the symptoms associated with stress. There *is* agreement within the scientific community about the damaging impact of continuously high stress levels on people. So, again, the organization, by its policy, has subjected its employees to a known health hazard (stress) in its attempts to minimize the exposure of its employees to what is only a possible hazard (radiation).

Clearly this is not an easy issue to resolve. No one wants to possibly expose an employee to radiation danger. Yet there is no confirmation that VDTs are such a threat; most scientific study has, in fact, concluded just the opposite. There remains, however, a natural hesitancy over this research. Too many times we have seen situations that were declared to be safe, later be proven to have been unsafe all along. We automatically wonder if VDT's will turn out to be another example of this.

On the other hand, as we have seen, a high level of mental and physical stress is a known threat to health. So one must ensure that possible solutions to the fear of radiation are not more stressful than the fear itself.

One way to begin to resolve this apparent dilemma is to step away from the specific issue of radiation and examine what should be done for all threats to health. Most organizations have a policy regarding industrial safety and most, if not all, union contracts spell out how safety issues are to be resolved. While not perfect, these provide a basis from which to proceed.

The broader issue, in fact, is employee safety, not radiation. And because the safety is determined by managing threats to both physical and mental well-being, the employee is the best judge of his or her own safety. When an employee begins experiencing symptoms that cause concern for personal health, that employee should have a way to evaluate the threat and to decide on a method for reducing it. The most common way is to consult with a knowledgeable medical practitioner, whether in-house or independent. If this source agrees that the symptoms are caused by the job, then steps should be taken to redress the situation. It is important that the organization have a standardized way of dealing with all such cases and that the outcome not be pre-determined by the specific situation.

By having such a policy in place, the organization demonstrates its concern for employees without raising concerns where perhaps none are needed. For example, one large organization has a policy that any person who feels his or her well-being is jeopardized takes the case to the medical doctor. The doctor is empowered to order changes in work location or work design if the health of the employee would be jeopardized by not doing so. The employee is not to be punished, through pay reduction or negative appraisal, for using this system.

This policy is used in many different ways. Some individuals are allergic to smoke. So, if through changes in assignment one were to be placed next to a smoker, the doctor can order a change in job location to protect the health of the allergic person. If a woman becomes pregnant and is concerned that working at a VDT will endanger her child, the doctor will discuss the problem, known evidence and possibilities with her. If she is still worried, the doctor can order changes in job assignment for the duration of the pregnancy to protect her from the harmful consequences of stress associated with the fear. Note that in this case, the organization does not publicly support the view that working at VDTs is bad. The organization, instead, recognizes that mental stress has severe negative consequences and must be dealt with on its own.

In this organization, each problem is seen as an individual one and each person is seen as responsible for managing his or her own health. The standard policy is that each person with a concern must take the initiative to consult with the medical staff to resolve any concerns. The organization will support such efforts, but does not assume that it knows what constitutes a health threat in every case. This organization, by the way, is very successful, is rated as extremely well-managed, and is considered by its competitors to be an innovative, flexible company to be feared in the marketplace. Concern for employees and the provision of policies such as discussed here are not "coddling" and have been proved many times to be success factors in organizations.

The solution presented may not work for every company. But the concept of disengaging the issue from the rhetoric is a valid one. Organizations are frequently accused of demonstrating their lack of concern for employees if they do not immediately act upon stories of unsafe environments. But management is rarely the Simon Legree painted by its detractors. Rather, complex issues are too often oversimplified and dealt with piecemeal rather than as complete problems. The result is the unexpected rise in other unsafe environments because of the lack of understanding of how interrelated the concepts of job design, physical design and health really are.

In addition to the worries over the straightforward physical effects and the possible radiation threat of VDTs, there is a third concern relating to the use of VDTs. This centers on the evidence that television watching can have undesirable neurological consequences for some viewers. The question is whether this impact is also found for those working with a cathode ray screen, since it uses the same technology as the television.

Merrelyn and Fred Emery, researchers at the Australian National University at Canberra, have expressed concern over this issue for many years and much of what we know is a result of their efforts. Even so, we still don't have enough information about this problem. The needed research is only now underway. But what has been discovered about the impact of television should be understood. A most interesting finding is that television viewing is known to precipitate, in a certain percentage of the population, a type of epilepsy known as photosensitive epilepsy. Estimates of those affected range from the more conservative 1 in 15,000 to the broader range which defines the at-risk population as 1 in 10 for adults and up to 1 in 3 for children. Because the epileptic seizures tend to be of the "petit mal", or mild, variety, they are not recognized as such by the person or by the people around. These seizures can only be confirmed by brainwave testing. Most often the behavior seen is drowsiness, which has been assumed, in our culture, to be the result of the content of the television programs. Yet the content of the programs is irrelevant; it is the light radiating from the screen that is thought to be responsible.

As serious as these tentative findings are, there are other suspicions regarding television that cause further concern. It has been shown that watching television induces a brainwave pattern consistent with sensory deprivation. In this case, TV can be seen to act like a drug by causing an "asleep while awake" condition. Again, the issue is not the content of the TV program; rather, after habituation, it can be demonstrated that, for many people, the condition sets in within seconds of sitting in front of the screen.

This finding may help explain why television has never achieved the expected results in the area of education. It has been found that TV is best for imparting very brief bits of information as opposed to in-depth understanding. Viewers are found to recognize the information if presented again, but not to remember it unaided. Information read off the screen is less likely to be learned by the reader than is the same information presented on paper.

We need to know a great deal more about whether the research into the impact of television screen viewing is applicable to VDT screens as well. Computer-based education has been promoted as a growth industry; perhaps it will suffer the same fate as did television-based education. Also, if errors are less likely to be seen when displayed on a screen rather than on paper or read from a dial, then the work done on a screen-based system may be less accurate. For example, when I discussed the problem with other writers who use computers or word processors in their work, we are all struck by the fact that using the machines has helped us tremendously in terms of enhancing creativity in writing. But most have noticed that our ability to edit the work is very much slower and much less accurate than when we edit printed pages.

Perhaps the introduction of alternate types of screens will solve some of the problems inherent in the older technology. One such alternative is the plasma-based screen, which employs a technology different from the cathode ray tube. Also, there are systems that use no screens; instead, they print out every line typed. Admittedly this is a slower way to work, but there may be instances where accuracy is so important that the loss of speed is justified.

The relationship between the implementation process, job design, physical design of space, management style and their impact on the physical and psychological well-being of employees is a complex one. In your own business, with all the information that will be gathered during

implementation and beyond, it is important to understand the relationship between symptoms, as reported or observed, and the possible issues
underlying the symptoms. If you don't, you'll probably end up attacking
the symptoms, the underlying issues will continue to cause problems and
management will be faced with the cost of dealing with symptoms without experiencing all of the benefits obtainable when issues are resolved.

While it is true that legislation and employment agreements will increasingly reduce the amount of freedom management has in dealing
with the introduction of new technology, each organization will respond
to these issues differently, in ways related to its own culture and level of
maturity. But there is no doubt that each will have to deal with the health
and safety issues if it is to achieve the benefits of using new tools.

EPILOGUE

Beyond Tomorrow

The topics this book has addressed so far are, generally, within the capacity of the individual organization and the people within it to handle. But, there are other issues which, though terribly important, are beyond the capacity of any one organization to deal with independently. In some instances these dilemmas are directly tied to the introduction of technology; in others technology will merely be an exacerbating force.

These societal issues are many. I'll mention a few of them here to demonstrate what I mean, and return to some for further discussion later in the chapter. One issue that will affect our entire society is the evolution of organizational form and function in such a way that there are fewer jobs available. Yet society has not evolved to a point where a person without a job is seen as a productive member — indeed, the unemployed feel that they have no identity. How do we create a society in which productive contribution is not synonymous with work and one's identity is not necessarily tied to one's job?

Also, this new form of organization requires and supports much looser ties with its employees. Its boundaries are less rigid and people move back and forth from being employed to not being employed. Yet financial arrangements, especially pensions and benefits, are not changing quickly enough to support such an arrangement. Who is responsible for ensuring that people have the benefits and security they need to function?

Another issue is the fact that society is moving from its industrial base to an information base more quickly than its members can gain the skills needed to function in this new environment. Who is going to train all of society's members? And who will pay the bill?

Consideration of these and similar issues quickly brings home the fact that there is much change that is going on that is beyond the scope of any one organization to handle. But, just because no one organization can independently resolve an issue is no reason to ignore it. The modern organization must be very sensitive to its environment and attempt to influence it to the degree possible. Industry lobbying groups, professional associations and labor alliances are useful in helping management and employees to have input on issues that are societal in scope. The proactive organization will usually fare better than the reactive one in this turbulent new world in which we live.

Changing the Definition of "Work"

We have all been brought up to equate what we do with what we are. "What will you *be* when you grow up?" is asked frequently of every child. The implication is that in order to "be", one must have a profession. At every conference, attendees are given name tags on which their title and perhaps organization too are listed. Those with "nothing" after their names are not taken very seriously.

There is considerable doubt, however, that this way of relating to the world can continue. Historically, it has not been the norm. Family lineage was much more important than profession. The fascination with "occupational lineage" is an artifact of the Industrial Society and will become obsolete as we leave it. Unfortunately, we are the one who must live through the pain that comes with changing our ways.

During the upheaval of adjusting to the new technology and new global markets there will be many people who are unemployed or seriously underemployed. We are already seeing the emergence of demands that the available work be shared, either through shorter work weeks or other means. As long as we cling to the old belief that what we do is who we are, then those who are not "doing", as defined by paychecks, will press for work. The social cost of ignoring this need to have a work identity is very high in terms of stress, suicides, child abuse, and other forms of physical violence and alienation.

Increasingly we are seeing challenges to this way of viewing the world. Those who have grown up in the last thirty years are less likely to equate work with self. They are more apt to be seeking ways to increase the overall quality of their life, with work being only a piece. This attitude will be very helpful to them in a society where the concept of work is no longer tied to the concept of productive contribution.

The value of unpaid work — whether motherhood, volunteer work, hobbies, support of the arts or going to school — will need to be seen as being of value to the society as a whole. Only by encouraging increasing numbers of people to hold this view can we hope to avoid severe societal dislocation.

A number of solutions have been proposed to help the transition. One is to guarantee a level of income which allows every member of society to live in an acceptable manner. This demonstration that society values its members for more than their "work" contribution helps disassociate being "unemployed" from being "unproductive".

Guaranteeing a job, via mandatory work sharing as mentioned above, is another solution. Unfortunately, this is very much grounded in the old belief that having a job is what makes you important. So this solution will not go very far in helping establish new attitudes. Still, in terms of easing the pain for those of the old belief system, it is one possible approach.

There are many other approaches to the issue. The point is that each organization and each individual has to become aware of the issues and the fundamental problems that must be addressed. Then they can participate in devising responses to ensure that the solutions (and there will be more than one) that are finally arrived at reflect the input of all involved parties.

Retraining for the Information Age

We know that within ten to twenty years everyone will have to be comfortable with using computer-based technology. Every day we see new uses for it introduced. For the time being, most applications are presented, to the public, as choices. For example, automated tellers are available, but for those who do not choose to use them, there are still some live tellers in the banks. Some hotels are now experimenting with the use of terminals to make your own reservations. And many airports have automatic ticketing machines. It is only a matter of time before some of the choices are removed and one will be forced to use the technology if one wants to have access to that service. This happened with the phone system when the dial system was introduced. The economies of automation are such that this process appears inevitable and seems to fulfill the desires of the majority.

What, then, is to become of the more than three billion people who were in existence before the computer revolution got rolling? They were educated in the traditional patterns and need a new skill. The challenge of bringing "computer literacy" to an entire population cannot be left to employers alone.

Small businesses, volunteer organizations, and many others cannot afford to retrain all of their employees. Large organizations, who may have more resources, cannot afford to provide training, only to have their people hired away by those who cannot train. And there are many, many people who are not currently employed — who is responsible for training them? People who will retire in the next five years will still be very much alive in twenty years — how are they to cope?

It will be important for organizations to begin influencing this debate as soon as possible. Many solutions are suggested, including tax incentives, government-supported adult education programs, and the like. Which is in the best interest of the majority without sacrificing the minority? To ignore the debate is to lose the opportunity to help develop a response that furthers personal and organizational goals.

I have argued many times in this book for organizations to aim toward flexibility and creativity as accepted patterns of behavior. These goals are inhibited both by excessive regulation and by the lack of skilled resources. So the resolution of this training issue is not a trivial problem for most companies and the individuals within them.

Providing Security to Individuals

Societal responses to the changing environment will need to include a new look at pensions and, in particular, the portability of pensions. Currently pensions provide a "golden handcuff" which keeps employees, in which the organization has invested many years, from leaving. However, in the future, for the good of both the organization and the individual, people will need to be able to move in and out of organizations and in and out of the working world with greater ease.

Pension reform must be considered to ensure that those who leave are not punished for doing so. Conversely, organizations must not experience punitive rules or taxes that reduce their ability to develop and evolve as needed in the future. It is not an easy problem to solve, but it must be tackled.

Additionally, the whole area of security (both pension and benefits) with respect to those who work parttime or from home needs to be examined. Currently, in most instances, people who work in non-traditional patterns are not covered by company benefit plans. To date, these people have often been marginal workers, adding a second income and covered by their spouses' benefits, or fairly powerless groups unable to negotiate a better deal. But this will not be the case in the future. More and more people will be considered contract workers and under current plans most would not have any right to benefits. They will not tolerate this lack. And rightly so, the societal impact of large numbers of workers without health, life and pension benefits is immense.

The transition phase in which we find ourselves will challenge us for quite a while. Unions, governments, organizations, and, most importantly, individuals, will need to work together to discover the actions that will resolve the many issues faced. Just as new values of collaboration and cooperation are replacing the value of competition in successful organizations, so too will these values become more important in the society as a whole. We cannot deal with the issues either as individuals or as if the issues were separate and unrelated. Joint decisionmaking and joint action will be the sources of success in helping us through the transition.

Transitions are always a time of disturbance. The old ways are no longer working, but the new ones are not yet discovered or widely held. So it is hard to know whether an option will bring you closer to a desired goal. And when an option *appears* not to be a way forward, how do we know if it is a detour or a dead end? There are no easy answers. There will be a period of overlap when new ways and old ways are both vying for dominance. Those who find success in exploring the new ways must show compassion for those who cling to the old. By definition, not everyone can be on the leading edge; so those fortunate enough to have realized where the forces of technology, economics and demographics are taking us (and to have guessed correctly — not an easy task) must not take advantage of their position to the detriment of others. The short-run success you may experience will be more than nullified by the long-term negative outcomes that we, as a society will realize. It is futile to strive to be a successful organization in a society that is not.

Notes

1. G. Bylinsky, "The Race to the Automated Factory", *Fortune*, Feb. 21, 1983, p. 54.
2. D. Yankelovich, *New Rules: Searching for Self-fulfillment in a World Turned Upside Down*, Bantam Books, Inc., 1982, p. 8.
3. E. Trist, "Adapting to a Changing World", *Presentation at the 6th International Personnel Conference*, Montreal, Canada, 1977.
4. United Steelworkers of America, *Towards a Trade Union QWL Agenda*, 1982.
5. "The Microchip Battleground", Canadian Broadcasting Corporation, 1983, pp.1-2.
6. *ibid.*, p. 5.
7. *ibid.*, p. 6.

Source Notes and Further Readings

What follows is a rather informal presentation of further readings which may be of interest and the various sources of information from which I have drawn my inspiration and theoretical foundation. This book was deliberately written with the minimum of footnotes, but that is not to say that its ideas and suggested approach have sprung full-blown from my imagination.

A constant dilemma for me was to present, in as direct and informal a style as possible, theories and ideas that, in the orginal, were often presented in a much more academic manner. For those who have become interested in learning more about certain areas, these notes will direct you to original sources (when published), so that you may continue your learning process.

Part One: The New Realities

In these two chapters, a number of sources were drawn on. As far back as 1965, Eric Trist and Fred Emery were alerting us to the fact that our work environment was changing in new and different ways (F. E. Emery, and E. L. Trist, "The Causal Texture of Organizational Environment," *Human Relations*, 18, (1965), pp. 21-32.) Other writers in this area include Peter Drucker (*Managing in Turbulent Times*. New York: Harper and Row, 1980), Robert Russel (*Office Automation: Key to the Information Society*. Montreal: The Institute for Research on Public Policy, 1981), Daniel Yankelovich (*New Rules: Searching for Self-fulfillment in a World Turned Upside Down*, Bantam Books, 1982.), Robert Reich (*The Next American Frontier*. New York: Times Books, 1982) and John Naisbitt (*Megatrends*. New York: Warner Books, Inc., 1982).

For more detail on the effect of the Baby Boom in the U.S., see R. Easterlin, *Birth and Fortune* (New York: Basic Books, 1980). The effect in Canada is described in J. Kettle, *The Big Generation* (Toronto: McClelland and Stewart, 1980).

Scientific Management theories are presented in F. Taylor, "The Principles of Scientific Management," in *Scientific Management* (New York: Harper & Row Publishers, 1947). An alternative approach is presented by the sociotechnical systems approach as represented in E. Trist, "The Evolution of Sociotechnical Systems," in A. Van DeVen and W. Joyce, *Perspectives on Organizational Design and Behavior* (New York: Wiley, 1981 and in W. Pasmore, and J. Sherwood (eds.) *Sociotechnical Systems: A Sourcebook* (La Jolla, California: University Associates, 1978). Much of the approach discussed in the text is derived from this sociotechnical approach to organizational management.

The notion of organizational "fit" as discussed in Chapter Three is based on a paper written by my colleagues Hans van Beinum and Ingrid Ljungberg-van Beinum called "Organization Development: A Matter of the Warp and the Weft" (unpublished, 1974.) Their analysis is based on work by Fred Emery but the reference was not given. For more on the relation between culture and strategy see H. Schwartz, and S. Davis, "Matching Corporate Culture and Business Strategy," *Organizational Dynamics*, Summer, 1981.

Part Two: Managing the Transition

Until recently there have not been many books available for those interested in understanding how to introduce new office technology in an effective, humane manner. Two of the earliest books were R. Uhlig, D. Farber and J. Bair, *The Office of the Future*, (Amsterdam: North Holland Publishing, 1979) and E. Mumford and M. Weir, *Computer Systems in Work Design — the ETHICS Method*, (London: Halsted Press, 1979). More recently introduced have been D. Tapscott, *Office Automation: A User-Driven Method* (New York: Plenum Publishing, 1982) and C. Pava, *Managing New Office Technology: An Organizational Strategy* (New York: The Free Press, 1983).

Articles are more numerous and more easily available to most readers. For example, see N. Margulies, and L. Colflesh, "A Socio-Technical Approach to Planning and Implementing New Technology," *Training and Development Journal*, December, 1982, pp. 16-29; J. Taylor, "Integrating Computer Systems in Organization Design," *National Productivity Review*, Spring, 1982, pp. 218-27; W. Kraus, and N. Weiler, "Overcoming Human and Organizational Barriers to Implementation of New

Technology," in R. Ritvo and A. Sargent (eds.) *The NTL Manager's Handbook* (Arlington, Virginia: NTL Institute, 1983); and A. Dowling, "Do Hospital Staff Interfere with Computer System Implementation?," *Health Care Management Review*, Fall, 1980, pp. 23-32.

Senior management's role in understanding and making organizational choices with respect to the introduction of new office technology is discussed in R. Walton, "Social Choice in the Development of Advanced Information Technology," in H. Kolodny and H. van Beinum (eds.) *The Quality of Working Life and the 1980's* (New York: Praeger, 1983); R. Walton, and W. Vittori, "New Information Technology: Organizational Problem or Opportunity?," *Office: Technology and People*, 1983, pp. 249-73, and H. van Beinum, "Organizational Choice and Micro-electronics," *QWL Focus*, August, 1981, pp. 1-6.

The list of organizational issues to be evaluated during the introduction of new technology was originally developed by Trigon Systems Group in 1982 for use by the Canadian Department of Communications for the evaluation of their field trials. The instrument used to collect the data on which the case in Chapter 6 is based was the Job Diagnostic Survey developed by and discussed in J. Hackman, and G. Oldham, *Work Redesign* (Reading, Massachusetts: Addison Wesley, 1980). One organization's experience with developing an integrated approach to introducing technology is presented in M. Donlevy's, "Assessing Organizational Impacts of New Computer Systems," (unpublished Master's thesis, Pepperdine University, April, 1984).

A useful booklet summarizing many of the issues involved in implementing new systems, is J. Mansell, and T. Rankin, "Changing Organizations: The Quality of Working Life Process," working paper no. 4, Ontario Quality of Working Life Centre, September, 1983.

The graphics used in this section were developed by Terry Golbeck for his unpublished paper, "Implementing Computer-based Technologies: Rationale for Employee Involvement."

Part Three: Managing the Integrated Office

Many of the earlier cited articles and books also deal with the issues raised in Parts Three and Four. I will only cite previously unmentioned contributions here.

Regarding new ways of managing, Harold Bridger presents a good overview of the skills needed in "The Relevant Training and Development of People for O. D. Roles in Open Systems," in K. Trebesch (ed.), *Organization Development in Europe* (Bern, Switzerland: Haupt, 1980, pp. 739-54. Other useful articles include R. Kanter, "The Middle Manager as Innovator," *Harvard Business Review*, July-August, 1982, pp. 95-105 and C. Argyris, "Double Loop Learning in Organizations," *Harvard Business Review*, September-October, 1977, pp. 115-25.

The transcript that is quoted several times in the text is an eye-opening experience for anyone who has not dealt directly with the "victims" of new technology. It is of the *Ideas* broadcast called *The Microchip Battleground* (4-ID-031, March 25 – April 7, 1983) and can be purchased directly from CBC Transcripts, P. O. Box 500, Stn. A, Toronto, Ontario, M5W 1E6.

An in-depth and quite revealing discussion of the social effects of communicating through computers is given in S. Hiltz, and M. Turoff, *The Network Nation: Human Communication via Computer* (Reading, Massachusetts: Addison-Wesley Publishing, 1978). Other aspects of job design are treated by S. Zuboff, "Psychological and Organizational Implications of Computer-Mediated Work," *Dissent*, December, 1981 and J. Main, "Work Won't Be the Same Again," *Fortune*, June 28, 1982.

The whole issue of working from home has just begun to be explored. Some interesting aspects are discussed in W. Renfro, "Second Thoughts on Moving the Office Home," *The Futurist*, June 1982, pp. 43-48, and in J. Applegath, *Working Free: Practical Alternatives to the 9 to 5 Job* (New York: AMACOM, 1982).

The physical design of space is an important topic and much has been written about its relation to new technology lately. Finding articles that integrate the design of space and the other human issues discussed earlier is less easy. Two interesting ones are G. Davis, and F. Szigeti, "Programming, Space Planning and Office Design," *Environment and Behavior*, May, 1982, pp. 299-317 and G. Davis, and I. Altman, "Territories at the Work-Place: Theory into Design Guidelines," *Man-Environment Systems*, January, 1976, pp.46-53. IBM publishes a useful little booklet called *Ergonomics Handbook* (IBM, SV04-0224-00). Also see F. Steele, *Physical Settings and Organizational Development* (Reading, Massachusetts: Addison-Wesley, 1973).

Part Four: The Key Human Resource Issues

Again, I will only cite those writings that have not been previously mentioned.

Training could be a book unto itself. For a view on the distinction between training and education see G. Bronsema, and P. Keen, "Education Intervention and Implementation in MIS," *Sloan Management Review*, Summer, 1983, pp. 35-43.

The evolution in work and careers is aptly described and discussed in C. Handy, "The Changing Shape of Work," *Organizational Dynamics*, Autumn, 1980, pp. 26-34 and in M. Olson, "Remote Office Work: Changing Work Patterns in Space and Time," *Communications of the ACM*, March, 1983, pp. 182-87.

The National Institute for Occupational Safety and Health (NIOSH) has been tracking health effects of office automation for several years and updated reports are issued regularly. The section on the relation between VDTs and epilepsy is based on research being conducted by Merrelyn and Fred Emery, which is an extension of earlier work into the effects of television. Articles include M. Emery, and F. Emery, "The Vacuous Vision: The TV Medium," *Journal of the University Film Association*, Winter-Spring, 1980, pp. 27-32; M. Emery, "The Role of the Mass Media in Nutrition Education," *Journal of Food and Nutrition*, 1982, pp. 94-107 (in which, despite the seemingly unrelated title, numerous relevant ethical issues are raised); and M. Emery, "Television Epilepsy", unpublished, 1982.

Bibliography

Applegath, J., *Working Free: Practical Alternatives to the 9 to 5 Job*. New York: AMACOM, 1982.

Argyris, C., "Double Loop Learning in Organizations," *Harvard Business Review*, September-October, 1977, pp. 115-25.

van Beinum, H. "Organizational Choice and Micro-electronics," *QWL Focus*, August, 1981, pp. 1-6.

van Beinum, H. and I. Ljungberg-van Beinum, "Organization Development: A Matter of the Warp and the Weft" (unpublished, 1974).

Bridger, H., "The Relevant Training and Development of People for O. D. Roles in Open Systems," in K. Trebesch (ed.), *Organization Development in Europe*. Bern, Switzerland: Haupt, 1980, pp. 739-54.

Bronsema, G. and P. Keen, "Education Intervention and Implementation in MIS," *Sloan Management Review*, Summer, 1983, pp. 35-43.

Davis, G. and I. Altman, "Territories at the Work-Place: Theory into Design Guidelines," *Man-Environment Systems*, January, 1976, pp. 46-53.

Davis, G. and F. Szigeti, "Programming, Space Planning and Office Design," *Environment and Behavior*, May, 1982, pp. 299-317.

Donlevy, M., "Assessing Organizational Impacts of New Computer Systems," unpublished Master's Thesis, Pepperdine University, April, 1984.

Dowling, A., "Do Hospital Staff Interfere with Computer System Implementation?," *Health Care Management Review*, Fall, 1980, pp. 23-32.

Drucker, P. F., *Managing in Turbulent Times*. New York: Harper and Row, 1980.

Easterlin, R., *Birth and Fortune*. New York: Basic Books, 1980.

Emery, F. E. and E. L. Trist, "The Causal Texture of Organizational Environment," *Human Relations*, 18, (1965), pp. 21-32.

Emery, M., "The Role of the Mass Media in Nutrition Education," *Journal of Food and Nutrition*, 1982, pp. 94-107.

Emery, M., "Television Epilepsy", unpublished, 1982.

Emery, M., and F. Emery, "The Vacuous Vision: The TV Medium," *Journal of the University Film Association*, Winter-Spring, 1980, pp. 27-32.

Ergonomics Handbook, IBM, SV04-0224-00.

Hackman, J. and G. Oldham, *Work Redesign*. Reading, Massachusetts: Addison-Wesley, 1980.

Handy, C., "The Changing Shape of Work," *Organizational Dynamics*, Autumn, 1980, pp. 26-34.

Hiltz, S. and M. Turoff, *The Network Nation: Human Communication via Computer*. Reading, Massachusetts: Addison-Wesley Publishing, 1978.

Kanter, R., "The Middle Manager as Innovator," *Harvard Business Review*, July-August, 1982, pp. 95-105.

Kettle, J. *The Big Generation*. Toronto: McClelland and Stewart, 1980.

Kraus, W. and N. Weiler, "Overcoming Human and Organizational Barriers to Implementation of New Technology," in R. Ritvo and A. Sargent (eds.) *The NTL Manager's Handbook*. Arlington, Virginia: NTL Institute, 1983.

Main, J., "Work Won't Be the Same Again," *Fortune*, June 28, 1982.

Mansell, J. and T. Rankin, "Changing Organizations: The Quality of Working Life Process," working paper no. 4, Ontario Quality of Working Life Centre, September, 1983.

Margulies, N. and L. Colflesh, "A Socio-Technical Approach to Planning and Implementing New Technology," *Training and Development Journal*, December, 1982, pp. 16-29.

The Microchip Battleground, broadcast on *Ideas* Series, (4-ID-031, March 25 – April 7, 1983) CBC Transcripts, 1983.

Mumford, E. and M. Weir, *Computer Systems in Work Design — the ETHICS Method*. London: Halsted Press, 1979.

Naisbitt, J., *Megatrends*. New York: Warren Books, Inc. 1980.

Olson, M., "Remote Office Work: Changing Work Patterns in Space and Time," *Communications of the ACM*, March, 1983, pp. 182-87.

Pasmore, W. and J. Sherwood (eds.) *Sociotechnical Systems: A Sourcebook*. La Jolla, California: University Associates, 1978.

Pava, C., *Managing New Office Technology: An Organizational Strategy*. New York: The Free Press, 1983.

Reich, R., *The Next American Frontier*. New York: Times Books, 1982.

Renfro, W., "Second Thoughts on Moving the Office Home," *The Futurist*, June, 1982, pp. 43-48.

Russel, R., *Office Automation: Key to the Information Society*. Montreal, Quebec: The Institute for Research on Public Policy, 1981.

Steele, F., *Physical Settings and Organizational Development*. Reading, Massachusetts: Addison-Wesley, 1973.

Schwartz, H. and S. Davis, "Matching Corporate Culture and Business Strategy," *Organizational Dynamics*, Summer, 1981.

Tapscott, D., *Office Automation: A User-Driven Method*. New York: Plenum Publishing, 1982.

Taylor, J., "Integrating Computer Systems in Organization Design," *National Productivity Review*, Spring, 1982, pp. 218-27.

Taylor, J., "Integrating Computer Systems in Organization Design," National Productivity Review, Spring, 1982, pp. 218-27.

Trist, E., "The Evolution of Sociotechnical Systems," in A. Van DeVen and W. Joyce, *Perspectives on Organizational Design and Behavior*. New York: Wiley, 1981.

Uhlig, R., D. Farber and J. Bair, *The Office of the Future*. Amsterdam: North Holland Publishing, 1979.

Walton, R., "Social Choice in the Development of Advanced Information Technology," in H. Kolodny and H. van Beinum (eds.) *The Quality of Working Life and the 1980's*. New York: Praeger, 1983.

Walton, R. and W. Vittori, "New Information Technology: Organizational Problem or Opportunity?," *Office: Technology and People*, 1983, pp. 249-73.

Yankelovich, D., *New Rules: Searching for Self-fulfillment in a World Turned Upside Down*. New York: Bantam Books, 1982.

Zuboff, S., "Psychological and Organizational Implications of Computer-Mediated Work," *Dissent*, December, 1981.

Index